Code Green

Code **Green**

EXPERIENCES OF A LIFETIME

Melbourne · Oakland · London

Contents

The Author

Kerry Lorimer, Coordinating Author

Kerry Lorimer has worked and travelled in over 100 countries on all seven continents, and sailed most of the oceans in between.

She's hitchhiked through Africa, and sailed the Atlantic, Pacific, sub-Antarctic and around Cape Horn. She's been held hostage; felt the breath of whales and wild hyena; been surrounded by snack-happy sharks; salsaed through South America; and, due to a total lack of any sense of direction, has been lost in more places than she can count.

In 20 years as a green-hued travel junkie, she has guided and operated minimum-impact treks, tours and expeditions in South America, the Himalaya, Australia, Africa, the Middle East and Antarctica.

Since 1998 Kerry has run a Sydney-based business consulting to travel companies, tourism bodies and production houses on responsible tourism, expedition management, marketing and communications.

Her articles and images have been published in books, magazines and newspapers, including a number of Lonely Planet guides and coffee-table editions.

Acknowledgements

Thanks to my amazing family and friends for their unstinting support, especially my parents. Thanks go to Annalise Penfold, James Jeffrey, Christine Hoult, Julie McGlone, Alex Gray, Pete and Gwyn Carlisle, Richard I'Anson, Lee Atkinson, Tracey Leitch, Jo Harle, Kristen Dinsdale, Rob Purves, Richard Simon and Andrew Rich.

Thanks also to the many friends, colleagues and Lonely Planet authors who contributed to the contents of this book, particularly Richard Field, Giselle Radulovic, Philip Engelberts, Kris Madden, Bridhe McGroder, Rachel Alt, Karen Jacobs, Rod Griffith, Garry Weare and Adam Long. Warm thanks to Sarah Hoyland and Julie McIntosh at the Classic Safari Company, Justin Francis at responsibletravel.com, and all the operators who offered their help in compiling the information here. And thanks to Chris Rennie and the Lonely Planet folk who made this happen!

Foreword BY TONY WHEELER

Loved to death. These days that scary phrase gets tagged on to more and more travel possibilities. We scratch our heads and wonder just when Bali's Kuta or India's Goa morphed from a quiet surfer's escape or a laid-back hippy hangout into international resorts of wall to wall shops, restaurants and package hotels. Then we look towards the Himalaya and ponder when 'I've Climbed Everest Too' will be a common enough claim to warrant a T-shirt. Cities everywhere worry about how they're going to cope with ever-increasing flows of tourists while some, like Venice, have simply given up the struggle and become full-time theme towns, not just dependent upon tourism but non-existent without it.

At Lonely Planet sustainable and responsible have always been part of our vocabulary. Of course, in our early days they weren't simply lines on a checklist – those key words had yet to be irrevocably linked with tourism – but looking back at our earlier books it's clear that we realised from the start that making a connection to the places we visited was a vital part of the message we wanted our guidebooks to carry.

Today, more than ever, we're utterly convinced of the incredible importance of travel. Sure it's a major industry, the world's biggest economic activity according to many studies. In fact for many countries in the developing world it's more than just a key part of their economies, it's often the overwhelming part. But tourism is far more than meals on the table and money in the wallet. In recent years it's been underlined again and again that it's only through travelling, through meeting people, that we begin to understand that we're all sharing this world and all coming along for the ride, despite the barriers that governments, religions, and economic and political beliefs often seem to build up between us.

So how do we make that ride not just a quick fairground twirl, but something that's going to last for the long run, something we can enjoy for our travelling lives and pass on to our children and future generations? *Code Green* is a peek into a box full of sustainable travel possibilities. Just like those early guidebooks we're certainly not trying to tell you, 'this is what you must do'. We're much happier showing just how exciting sustainable travel can be and alerting you to the possibilities waiting to be explored.

In some cases it's going to be guidelines on how to tread softly; how to ensure that our footprints are faint ones. Or it might be accepting that what we're doing is going to have an impact, but at the same time ensuring we balance the negative with a positive. In other cases it's going to be waving the flag for places, activities and operations that are definitely worth trying. Surprisingly, sustainable can also mean comfortable or stylish, it can even include a touch of luxury.

Most important are the places where sustainable and tourism are inseparable, the first word simply couldn't be there without the second. In many cases – from African wildlife to whales – it's tourism that is the ultimate guarantor of a species' survival. Elephants may be perceived as nothing more than heavyweight crop tramplers if we can't manage to make them championship tourist attractions. In other situations tourism can provide a far more environmentally friendly income than anything else on offer. When the only income comes from turning ever more marginal mountain land into ever less viable subsistence farm acreage, it's clear that catering for trekkers and mountaineers can be a much more sensible alternative.

Today there's no way of avoiding the importance of travelling responsibly and with *Code Green* we hope to show how to make your next trip count.

Introduction

Every seasoned traveller has a story about a magical place they knew 20 years ago – the deserted beach, the remote mountain village – that has succumbed to rampaging development or has been 'ruined' by too many backpackers and package tourists.

If you've travelled in the developing world, at some point you've no doubt had a dose of traveller's guilt, stemming from the contrast between the poverty you witnessed around you and your relative wealth – and wished that you could do something to make a difference.

But if you think about your best travel experiences – the ones you'll never forget – they're almost always those where you made a *connection*. Where you were blown away by a landscape so magnificent in its scale and purity that you were at once humbled – and exquisitely aware of your own integral place in the natural order. Or when you felt you really made a personal connection – and felt an equality of give and take – with someone from a world utterly different to your own.

In a nutshell, *Code Green* is about travelling in a way that minimises your impact – and maximises those connections. And it's about making a difference and 'giving something back'.

Code Green is a glimpse into the world of 'responsible travel' – one we hope will inspire you to try a new, alternative approach to travelling.

Code Green is the antithesis of watching the world blur by through the bus window.

We're talking about taking new trails – or revisiting old favourites – in a 'sustainable' way; about getting under the skin of a country; engaging – equitably and respectfully – with local people and immersing yourself in the culture; about fair trade; about getting involved in local communities, perhaps as a volunteer; and about having the best travel experiences of your life.

We've included nearly a hundred inspiring responsible travel experiences from across the planet, ranging from independent travel to small group tours; grass-roots community organisations to large-scale international operators; and just a smattering of the huge and growing number of volunteer opportunities.

You'll get up-close-and-personal with gorillas in Rwanda, lemurs in Madagascar and sea lions in the Galápagos. You can explore some of the world's most magnificent wilderness, and see it through the eyes of the Dogon people of Mali, the Maasai of Kenya, the Maoris of New Zealand or the Inuit of Greenland. You can help tag turtles on the Great Barrier Reef, count macaws in Peru or learn to be a ranger in an Indian tiger sanctuary.

It's not all hardship and hair shirts – our examples range from basic budget backpacking through to the most sumptuous luxury. But every example adheres to the principles of responsible tourism: they are sensitive to environment and culture, and ensure that a proportion of their revenue is directed into the host community.

Not all of them are 'perfect' examples of responsible tourism – in fact, most aren't. With this nascent branch of the travel tree, everyone's still learning and improving. Neither are we claiming that those we've chosen are the 'best'.

However, all the examples in this book have been selected on the basis that they are striving to observe the principles of responsible travel, that they recognise their shortcomings and are working to shrink the gap between practice and perfection.

We've tried to select experiences that have some natural 'limiting force' – places that can benefit from some increased business but, whether through enforced park entry quotas, potential sustainable expansion, or other means, are in less danger of over-exploitation.

We hasten to add that this is a selection of ideas and directions to inspire you to find your own less-travelled path – if you follow it to the letter, you defeat its purpose.

There are also tips to help you make responsible travel choices: how to distinguish the good travel operators from the hucksters; true ecotourism from 'eco-lite' and how to develop your 'greenwash' radar. There's tips on how to cope with conscience-challenging issues such as begging, breaking the ice with local people and how to minimise your personal impact on wilderness. How do you offset the environmental cost of your fuel-guzzling, emission-blurting, long haul flight? Read on!

We hope all of this will give you the tools and the inspiration you need to try a new way of travelling – one that will challenge your perceptions, shake you out of your comfort zone, enthral you and enrich your soul. You'll not only make a contribution to other people's lives, you might just change your own.

What is 'Responsible Tourism'?

Ecotourism, responsible tourism… what's the difference and how can you tell the good guys from the greenwashers?

'Ecotourism' is described by the International Ecotourism Society (TIES) as 'responsible travel to natural areas that conserves the environment and improves the well-being of local people'.

The problem with 'ecotourism' is that there's no universally agreed-upon definition. Back in the 1980s and early 1990s when ecotourism really took off, everyone wanted a piece of the action and, without any regulatory control, a whole host of dodgy operators jumped on the bandwagon, to the extent that just about anyone with a four-wheel drive taking tours in the great outdoors was using the 'eco' label.

Not surprisingly, the term lost a lot of its currency.

Partly in reaction to the misuse of the ecotourism label, and partly in recognition that the principles of ecotourism could – and should – apply to all tourism, not just in natural areas, a new paradigm has emerged: responsible tourism.

Responsible tourism can be more-or-less defined as travel that takes into consideration the following 'triple bottom line' issues.

Environment Travel that minimises negative environmental impacts and, where possible, makes positive contributions to the conservation of biodiversity, wilderness, natural and human heritage. Where travellers and locals learn and share information, leading to better appreciation and understanding.

Social/Cultural Travel that respects culture and traditions and recognises the rights of all peoples to be involved in decisions that affect their lives and to determine their future. By involving and engaging local people, there is authentic interaction and greater understanding between travellers and hosts, which builds cultural pride and community confidence.

Economic Travel that has financial benefits for the host community and operates on the principles of fair trade. Monies spent by travellers remain in the community through the use of locally owned accommodation, staff and services; funding community initiatives, training or other in-kind support.

As a traveller, responsible tourism is about accepting responsibility for your actions, attitudes and impacts: through your conscious choices, you can minimise your personal impact and make a positive contribution. Be a part of the solution, rather than the problem.

In its best manifestations, responsible tourism can be a powerful tool for conservation of biodiversity and for sustainable development.

Here are a few tips for travelling responsibly.

- If travelling independently, try to minimise your personal environmental impact: there are more detailed checklists throughout this book, including carbon offset programmes (p128) and trail etiquette (p78).

- If you're travelling on a group tour, select operators and hotels that have – and abide by – a responsible tourism policy that addresses environmental and cultural issues, as well as making a financial contribution to community or environmental projects. And ask questions (there' s a checklist on p30).

- Try to avoid destinations that are already over-crowded, or travel in the off-season.

- Try to use locally owned hotels and services, eat in locally owned restaurants and use public transport where possible – it not only minimises your environmental impact, it means your money directly benefits the locals, and you'll generally have a far more enriching experience!

- Do unto others: treat local people with respect and you will be treated likewise. For further tips, see p178.

- Abide by the laws and regulations of the country you're in, particularly regarding natural resources like parks and waterways.

- Don't be tempted to buy souvenirs made from wild animal products, including skins, ivory or bone. Not only is it illegal to import or export such items, in most cases you're also likely to be supporting poaching practices that have had devastating impacts on animal populations. Similar principles apply to wooden products.

- Be aware of suggested or legal approach distances and other recommendations for observing wildlife. A basic rule of thumb is if the animal is altering its behaviour due to your presence, then you're too close.

BEFORE YOU LEAVE HOME

The more you know about a country and its people before you arrive, the more readily you get a handle on things and the quicker you slip under the skin of a place. With a little forward planning, you can make a significant difference – and your conscience will be cleaner and greener.

- **Do as much research as you can before you leave home. Destination guides provide specific tips, but novels, non-fiction and the Internet put flesh on the bones of this advice. The Internet is an amazing resource for background – check out the Lonely Planet Thorn Tree (http://thorntree.lonelyplanet.com) to read travellers' first-hand experiences and answer any questions.**

- **Learn a few phrases in the local language – even if it's just 'hello', 'thank you', and 'may I take your photo?' Even your most stumble-tongued efforts will be appreciated by the locals!**

- **Get acquainted with local customs – what's OK and what's not when you're eating and drinking with local people, acceptable social behaviour, religious practices, dress etc. Consider your choice of clothes and gear accordingly.**

- **Think about what, if any, gifts you might take. Something evocative of your own country usually works well. Work out the appropriateness of the gifts, to whom and in what situations they might be given.**

- **Try to leave excess packaging at home (eg film boxes, anything plastic you may need to dispose of). Developing countries generally don't have waste collection services, so your packaging will end up as their pollution. Take biodegradable soap and shampoo.**

- **Consider your transport options: could you ride a bike rather than drive, take a train rather than fly?**

- **Look at off-setting your contribution to carbon emissions, so your travels are 'carbon neutral'.**

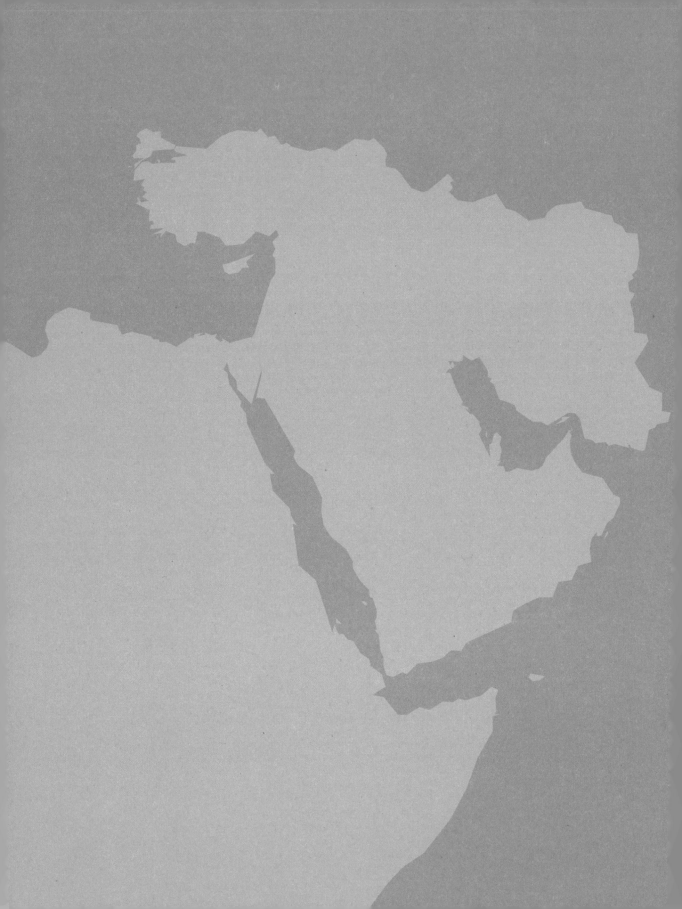

Africa & the Middle East

CAMEROON ~ BAMENDA HIGHLANDS:
SAVE A BIRD, HELP THE COMMUNITY

BY MARK ELLIOTT

Even among passionate twitchers, few have ever seen the Bannerman's turaco (*Tauraco bannermani*). This startled-looking bird with its curious punk-red mohawk quiff is only found in the Bamenda highlands of northwestern Cameroon. And then only within very specific mountain forests of the Kilum-Ijim ridge. Hugging volcanic Lake Oku, this beautiful virgin forest is the last remnant to fit the exacting habitat and altitude demands of the fussy bird. But it is also sandwiched between two vibrant human communities, Oku and Kom, whose population growth tempts them to cut down the forest for agricultural uses.

Bird-lovers realised that deforestation of the birds' unique ecosystem had to stop. But they also realised that this could not be achieved by declaring a closed reserve and alienating the local people. Supported since 1987 by Birdlife International, the Kilum-Ijim project's approach was to find the villagers alternative ways to improve their living standards without burning the trees. Cottage industries, notably honey gathering, developed while discussion-based education programmes persuaded locals that sustainably harvesting the forest was more valuable than burning it down for fields.

Tourism here remains an idea more than a reality; rare visitors are mostly limited to organised birding groups. Nonetheless, by agreement with the project managers, adventurous independent travellers can hire project workers as guides to navigate the forest paths, and can arrange accommodation at the project's clean, simple guesthouse in Oku. (It's worth writing in advance).

Even if you don't see a turaco, the colourful local cultures with their court hierarchies, juju spirit men and extraordinarily complex voodoo-esque superstitions makes this area a fascinating discovery.

ANTHONY HAM / LPI

RESPONSIBLE TRAVEL CREDENTIALS

- **The patronage of forest-appreciating foreigners – and the money they spend – strengthens locals' convictions of the value of conserving, rather than destroying, the forest and wildlife.**

- **Sustainably-produced local handicrafts, candles and honey make great gifts. Paper handmade from recycled scraps is crafted into stylish greetings cards in Oku village. These products are ready but await tourist buyers!**

- **By paying project staff to take you into the forest for bird-watching, you're also helping to fund their main task of patrolling the forest and monitoring poaching or illegal woodcutting. Thus you're helping to protect the birds you spot.**

WHEN TO GO

March is best for spotting a Bannerman's turaco and to avoid the heavy rains that obliterate views from May onwards.

GETTING THERE

Douala, Cameroon's biggest city, is served by international flights. Buses run daily to Bamenda from which Oku is approximately 2½ hours' drive via Banso (also known as Kumbo). Sporadic minibuses operate. The track to Oku can prove impassable in the rainy season.

Birding Africa organises specialist tours occasionally including the surrounding Bamenda highlands area, though not Oku village.

Communication difficulties mean that many visitors prefer to stay, at least initially, in Bamenda, where the acceptable Skyline Hotel (☎ 361289; from US$30) is well-placed on Bafoussam Rd overlooking town.

Oku has some simple shops, eateries and 'off-licenses' (simple pubs selling Guinness and Bière 33). Its one dance-spot plays superbly mellifluous Zingeh music.

Further information: Kilum-Ijim Forest Project, PO Box 275, Bamenda, Cameroon | **www.birdlife.org** | **www.birding-africa.com**

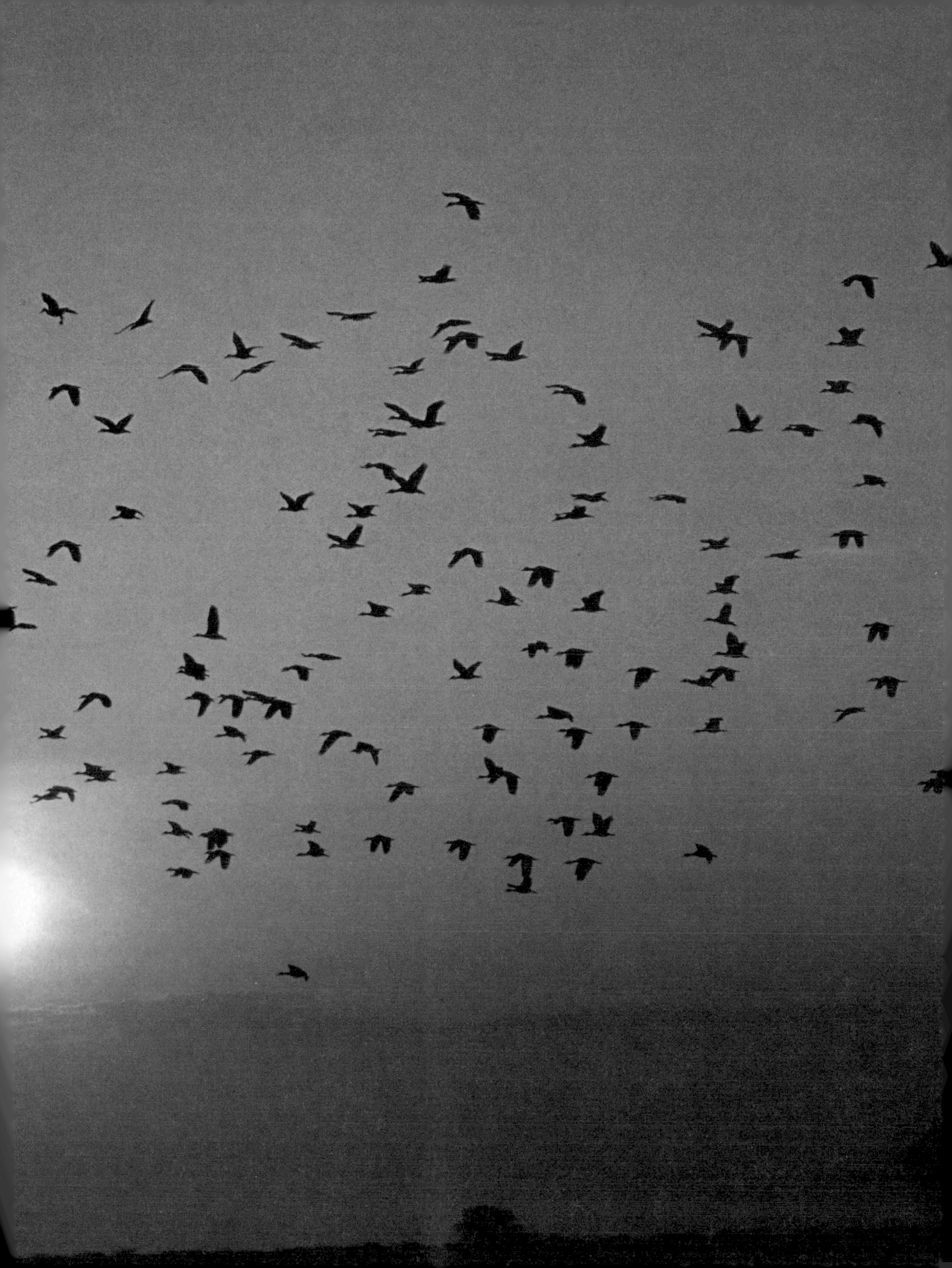

DUBAI ~ AL MAHA:
LAWRENCE OF ARABIA MEETS LUXURY
IN THE NAME OF CONSERVATION
BY KERRY LORIMER

TONY WHEELER | LPI

EMIRATES, COURTESY OF AL MAHA DESERT RESORT

If you want to achieve a conservation outcome against the odds, it helps if you have the blessing of a crown prince. Al Maha – a luxurious resort amid a desert reserve – was conceived by Emirates Airlines at the behest of the Crown Prince Of Dubai. Its development led to the creation of a national park (requiring a change to the country's constitution), which is now the largest wildlife reserve in the Middle East.

Established in 1999 as the project's first stage, the Al Maha Desert Resort is unadulterated opulence. 'Bedouin-style' suites are decked out with antiques; deluxe spa treatments and vintage champagne are *de rigueur*.

Three years later, after a major environmental audit, the resort's vice president and ecologist, Tony Williams, convinced Emirates and the government to enter into a $10 million partnership to fence off 5% of the emirate and proclaim it a national park.

The resulting 225-sq-km dubai desert Conservation Reserve now shelters desert foxes, gazelles and small numbers of endemic Arabian oryx (a large antelope until now threatened with extinction) as well as a range of rare and curiously-adapted fauna. Red-tawny sand dunes roll to the sunset à la *Lawrence of Arabia,* but now stands of native shrubs and bushes have been re-established, providing shelter for animals. It's a stark contrast to the camel-ravaged landscape beyond the perimeter fence.

While entry to the conservation area is available to anyone and a number of local operators offer tours, the resort's well-heeled clients have the advantage of staying inside the park: scimitar-horned oryx have been known to take a drink from guests' private swimming pools. Game drives, camel and horse treks, and traditional Arabian pursuits such as archery and falconry are included in the tariff.

RESPONSIBLE TRAVEL CREDENTIALS

- To integrate conservation needs with tourism, the reserve is divided into four sections, including a zone where no human intervention is allowed except by researchers, on foot.

- The resort runs on advanced energy and water recycling systems. Solar power is used wherever practical.

- Recycled water is used on the 6000 indigenous plants that have been reintroduced in one of the regions' largest reseeding programmes.

- Al Maha reintroduced a number of endangered and indigenous species – numbering some 200 animals – to the reserve. From the original 90 Arabian oryx, over 170 animals now roam throughout the reserve.

- Fifteen per cent of the resort's staff work full-time on conservation projects, which include ground-water research and reintroduction of endangered species.

- Resort activities keep alive the fast-disappearing traditional activities of the Bedouin, including falconry, camel and horseback dune safaris.

- Al Maha works with local camel farmers, encouraging best-practice techniques, as well as guiding farmers in their efforts to establish tourism services.

- The Al Maha self-supporting business model was designed to take the reliance on 'charity' out of conservation projects. it is now a highly successful and internationally recognised tourism and conservation model.

- Five per cent of profits go towards conservation programmes.

WHEN TO GO

The winter months, November to April, are the most pleasant. It is less humid than the city over summer. Activities are open year-round.

GETTING THERE

Al Maha is located 45 minutes from dubai and transfers can be arranged.

There are 40 suites, ranging in levels of air-conditioned sumptuousness, and in price from us$560 to us$2000 per night. All suites have a private swimming pool, come with a personal guest relations coordinator and field guide, and include all meals, activities and desert excursions.

Local Dubai-based tour operators run four-wheel-drive day trips to the less-restricted zones of the conservation area. Camel treks, sand-skiing and dining in bedouin tents are also offered. The park entry fee (US$5) goes to reserve and conservation work.

EGYPT ~ SOUTH SINAI: TREKKING WITH THE JABALIYA BEDOUIN

BY ANTHONY SATTIN

Most people head to Sinai for its beaches and amazing coral gardens and if they do leave the coast, it is usually only to climb 2244m-high Mt Sinai. A better understanding of the unique culture and environment of the Bedouin can be experienced by trekking the desert mountains and valleys of southern Sinai with the local Jabaliya.

The Jabaliya are a Bedouin tribe who claim descent from the Slav families brought to the desert by the Emperor Justinian in the 6th century to provide protection for monks and pilgrims at St Katherine's Monastery. The tribe's name means 'from the mountains', a terrain in which they are still at home, even though most now live a more settled village life.

An area of 4350 sq km around the monastery was turned into a national park in 1996 and has since been made a Unesco World Heritage site. It is visually stunning and sparsely populated: perfect for trekking. Its rich ecosystem supports varied wildlife, including hyenas, gazelles, ibex, lizards, vipers and a range of migrant birds.

The St Katherine's Protectorate has made a point of using the Jabaliya's expertise to help preserve the surrounding environment. Walking with the Jabaliya (camels are usually used to carry supplies, not people) is simply the best way of getting the most out of this unique experience and it helps sustain a community that lives, increasingly, on the tourist dollar.

MARK DAFFEY / LPI

RESPONSIBLE TRAVEL CREDENTIALS

- **For more than 1500 years the Jabaliya have had a free hand at managing the environment around St Katherine's, a task at which they have been uniquely successful.**

- **The Jabaliya have a monopoly on taking tourists up Mt Sinai and these longer-range treks help to foster better understanding between the Bedu and foreigners.**

- **The St Katherine Protectorate is a collaboration between an unusually diverse group, including the Greek Orthodox monks of the monastery, the Jabaliya Bedouin, the Egyptian government's National Parks department and the EU.**

WHEN TO GO

Summer days are blisteringly hot and winter nights are icy. Winds can be fierce in April.

GETTING THERE

You can fly to Sharm el Sheikh direct from several European cities or via Cairo. A daily bus runs from Cairo to Al Milga, the village near the monastery (six to eight hours).

Sheikh Musa at the Mountain Tours Office in Al Milga is one of the leading figures of the Jabaliya tribe and has use of some 400 camels and their owners. He can organise and equip tours from an overnight to a 10-day trek. Guides cost around US$9 a day, each camel costs US$9 a day, Sheikh Musa also charges a US$9 admin fee and food/utensils may also cost up to US$9 a day.

Sleeping options include the guesthouse of St Katherine's Monastery (☎ 2069 347 0353), which has rooms for US$55 for a double half-board (dinner B&B) and US$32 for a single, and the wonderful Al-Karn Ecolodge (☎ 2062 470 032), a small Bedouin-owned lodge 20km from St Katherine's, where solar power provides hot water but the lack of electric lights makes for great stargazing.

ETHIOPIA ~ LASTA & SIMIEN MOUNTAINS: TOUCHED BY ANGELS IN LALIBELA LABYRINTH

BY KERRY LORIMER

FRANCES LINZEE GORDON | LPI

KERRY LORIMER

Many think of Ethiopia as a land ravaged by civil war and famine. But it was once touched by angels. Legend has it that Saint George and a bevy of winged builders fast-tracked the construction of Bet Giyorgis, the perfectly-rendered Orthodox Christian church with its cruciform floor plan, which was liberated from Lalibela's bedrock in the 12th century.

Rather than building up, the incumbent King Lalibela – with divine assistance – did the opposite: he excavated. Bet Giyorgis is a free-standing monolith in a 12m pit: its roof is at ground level.

Descending worn stone steps, the mumble of pilgrim prayers and tendrils of incense – real frankincense – waft through the labyrinth of tunnels and trenches that connect the dozen or so rock-hewn churches that make up the Lalibela complex. Hereditary priests guard ancient treasures. Beggars beseech alms. Ascetic hermits inhabit grottoes in the walls, waiting to become piles of bones like those heaped in similar hollows.

Lalibela is isolated in the Lasta Mountains of Ethiopia. The air is thin at 2630m. But this is the veranda beneath the 'roof' of Africa. Further to the north, the Simien Mountains have 20 peaks over 4000m.

Some of Africa's best trekking is in the Simien Mountains National Park. Narrow tracks meet the edges of escarpments and dizzying drops where lammergeyers and vultures soar below. Camp sites are set beneath serrated skylines and overlook views that extend a hundred kilometres over the plains.

Accompanied by an entourage of mules, mule handlers, guides and camp staff, you'll share the trails with villagers and white-robed pilgrims on their way to the churches of Lalibela and Gondar. There's a good chance of bumping into troupes of gelada baboons (aka bleeding heart baboons for their red chest patches) and of catching fleeting glimpses of Simien foxes and walia ibexes – some of Africa's rarest animals.

Poor image and access have meant that Ethiopia is still below the radar for mainstream tourism. It will take foresight – and perhaps the touch of angels – to ensure the country's astonishing attractions are sustainably managed into the future.

RESPONSIBLE TRAVEL CREDENTIALS

- **Lalibela and the Simien Mountains National Park are both World Heritage–listed and managed by Unesco to ensure conservation of species and environment and sustainable management of tourism. Permits are required, as is an armed scout. One guide (a local) per six clients is also required by the park's board.**

- **Gate fees at Lalibela go towards maintenance of the churches.**

- **Using local trekking staff ensures monies return to communities in some of the country's remotest areas. Mule handlers, scouts and guides are rotated to ensure equitable employment.**

- **Tourism is seen as a major part of the solution to Ethiopia's post–civil war woes, and is expected to overtake coffee as the country's major export earner within five years.**

- **Currently, most of Ethiopia's tourism infrastructure is Ethiopian-owned, which gives the infant tourism industry a head start compared with other African countries.**

WHEN TO GO

The average temperature in Addis Ababa is 20°C, year-round. The rainy season is from mid-June to the end of September. Peregrine's trips run between October and January.

GETTING THERE

Peregrine Adventures operates a 14-day trip that incorporates an eight-day Simien Mountains trek and two days in Lalibela. It departs from the capital, Addis Ababa, and costs A$1995 plus A$365 for three internal flights. This includes most meals, camping equipment (dome tents), specialist guides, camp staff, hotels, transfers and entry fees.

FACING PAGE: A guide points from the summit of Mietgogo in Geech Camp to the panorama of the Simien Mountains.

Further information: www.peregrineadventures.com

GAMBIA & SENEGAL ~ ABENE: A THUMPING GOOD TIME ON THE ATLANTIC COAST

BY ANTHONY SATTIN

Not so long ago the playing of drums in West Africa was reserved for griots, the traditional praise singers, masters at making drums talk. But now you don't have to go far in Senegal or Gambia to find someone who will teach you. Individual lessons are inexpensive, but it is usually more fun to take part in a drum camp. In this week-long course of lessons, African drummers will coax a group of foreigners into rhythm.

The variety of drums is as unexpected as the range of sounds that can be created by banging a piece of wood, metal or a taut animal skin. *Seourouba*, *bougarabou*, *sabar*, *tamar*…each African drum has a name and a distinct character. And each has a role to play in local traditions and, increasingly, on the world stage. Drums are a key element in *mbalax*, the music of Senegalese singer Youssou N'Dour – the most prominent African presence at the 2005 Live8 concerts. *Mbalax* uses both the low, rhythmic beat of the *djembe* and the higher-octane, more intrusive sound of the *tamar*.

Tambacouda in Senegal and Brikama in Gambia both have strong music traditions and are good places to look for drum teachers who give individual or group lessons. The best option, though, is Abene in Senegal, both for its music tradition and for its setting – a small village on a beautiful stretch of the Atlantic coast.

Each December Abene stages a festival that attracts musicians and dancers from across the region. For the rest of the year it is a quiet village of family compounds grouped around a sacred tree, a big beach, some *campements* (fixed camps with little huts or bungalows), and a hall that occasionally serves as the nightclub. And if you are not woken in the morning by birds, you are likely to be roused by the sound of drummers impersonating birdsong.

DAVID TIPLING LIFI

RESPONSIBLE TRAVEL CREDENTIALS

- This is low-key, low-impact travelling, staying in traditional huts and spending time with villagers.

- West African society is changing rapidly and griot traditions are fading fast. Foreign interest in West African music has become one of the most influential forces for preserving this tradition.

- In a region of chronic unemployment and significant poverty, having music or dance lessons is an effective way of helping out, learning about local traditions and having a good time.

WHEN TO GO

December to April is the easiest time – after the rains (and therefore with less risk of malaria) and before the big heat.

GETTING THERE

Abene is a few miles from Gambia's southern border. Banjul is the nearest international airport, served by scheduled and charter flights. Buses and taxis cross the border into Casamance.

Many people in Abene, and elsewhere in Senegal and Gambia, teach drums as well as xylophone, kora and a range of other instruments, but you might have more fun joining a drum camp, such as at dancer Thomas Diabang's O'Dunbeye Land (£2.50 room only, £11.50 full board, £5.50 per dance or drum class).

Abene's *campements* range from basic huts in family compounds to comfortable rooms in mature gardens.

Further information: www.odunbeyeland.com | **http://djembelfaq.drums.org**

JORDAN ~ WADI MUJIB NATURE RESERVE: SPLASHING THROUGH A WET & WILD WADI

BY BRADLEY MAYHEW

I was hoping for third time lucky. Twice I'd travelled down through the sticky heat of Jordan's Dead Sea Hwy to the Wadi Mujib Nature Reserve and twice I'd met with a sad shake of the head: 'the group has cancelled'; 'water levels are too high'. This time, it was on.

I'd booked a hike along the reserve's Malaqi Trail through the responsible-tourism branch of the Royal Society of Conservation of Nature (RSCN), the NGO that operates Jordan's nature reserves. At US$57 for the day hike, it wasn't a cheap option, but I'd been assured that this was 'the most fun you could have in a single day in Jordan'. I tightened my flotation jacket and poked half-heartedly at a rappelling harness in a vain attempt to convey an impression of expertise. No-one was fooled.

As my guide, Ahmed, and I clambered up through the lush foliage of the wadi (a seasonal river bed), the hike was hot, sweaty and scratchy. After the initial weirdness of walking straight into a stream without first taking off my shoes ('We are Gore-Tex!', my shoes protested), we found ourselves pausing above a series of idyllic deep pools. We jumped into a deliciously cold rush, half-swimming, half-pulling ourselves along ropes, over boulders and up rushing rapids.

The towering canyon walls narrowed, the sunlight faded and the sky shrank to a sliver of blue, framed by sandstone cliffs and cut by the cries of swooping kingfishers. I floated downriver on my back, staring up at the wadi walls in a timeless moment of undiluted relaxation.

Then, gradually, the creek's background rush built to a roar and (after reaching for my proverbially absent paddle) I peered over the lip of a cliff and watched open-mouthed as the hiking route dropped 20m into a foaming waterfall. Ahmed set up the ropes, politely ignoring my half-stifled cry of 'Are you *kidding* me?', and before I knew it I was squatting over the edge of the fall, too scared to do what I knew I had to do: trust myself to Ahmed and the rope. Fighting all instincts of self-preservation I gradually lowered myself down into the spray and behind the fall, taking care not to touch the huge wall of water. The roar was deafening; the adrenalin intoxicating.

From here on it was a delicious float down the silent canyon. The water dropped gradually from my chest, to my waist, my knees and then my ankles, as the wadi walls opened and the visitors centre came into sight.

'That was *sooo* great!' I enthused, as I rang out my dripping socks. 'Can we do it again?'

RESPONSIBLE TRAVEL CREDENTIALS

- **Only 25 people are allowed on the Malaqi Trail per day to minimise the environmental impact.**

- **The RSCN trains and employs locals as rangers and guides and helps market locally-produced organic foods and handicrafts.**

- **The RSCN's responsible-tourism projects help fund the reintroduction of locally extinct and endangered species such as the Nubian ibex and the Arabian oryx.**

WHEN TO GO

The wadi is only safe between April and October, due to the danger of flash floods. The Dead Sea area can be very hot during these months.

GETTING THERE

Wadi Mujib Nature Reserve is a two- to three-hour drive from Jordan's capital, Amman.

There's no public transport to the reserve, so you'll have to hire a taxi or rent a car in Amman (around US$43 per day).

You can book accommodation at the reserve camp site, right on the shores of the Dead Sea, for around US$23 to US28 per person. Facilities include beds, showers and a restaurant. Private camping is not allowed.

The Malaqi Trail is a half-day hike, splash and rappell through the reserve that starts and finishes at the visitors centre.

Bring sunscreen, lots of drinking water, shoes that can get wet, a waterproof bag for your camera and valuables, a swimming costume and a towel.

KENYA ~ LEROGHI MOUNTAINS: JOURNEY WITH THE SAMBURU TO THE GREAT RIFT

BY KERRY LORIMER

Once upon a time, a Kenyan hunter-turned-conservationist named Peter Faull sat down with an old Ndorobo tribesman called Hitler and heard tales passed from his grandfather about a legendary elephant hunter from over the Leroghi Mountains on the eastern flank of the Great Rift Valley.

Hitler deputised a tribal Elder and medicine man, Lekermogo, to lead Faull on a journey through the montane forests and along the ridges of the remote Leroghi range in northern Kenya to the El Bogoi Valley, where they found the remains of the camp fires of Arthur H Neumann, explorer and hunter, who'd spent three years in the area in the 1890s.

Faull, Lekermogo and a team of Samburu and Ndorobo tribesmen now lead walking safaris that follow beast-forged trails through lush forests and sunny glades, periodically spitting forth trekkers onto the very edge of the Great Rift. From distinctive natural lookouts such as Nabolo Rock, plateaus and peaks extend to the north. To the west, vertiginous kilometre-deep drops meet broad savannah, stretching to blue-haze ranges on the far side of one of the world's greatest tectonic dividers.

Taking time to smell the flowers – and to learn a little of their botanical peculiarities – and to forego right of way to the odd large herbivore such as buffalo or elephant, the walks involve around four to six hours of hottish hiking per day.

Lekermogo heads up the team of 10 Samburu warriors who, along with the Faulls, run the logistical side of the expedition, as well as imparting tracking tips, legend and lore and an insight into the modern-day challenges faced by the traditional tribespeople of Kenya.

This is one of the most remote and rarely visited areas of Kenya, so meeting the Samburu villagers in a traditional *manyatta* (a cluster of dwellings under one chief) along the way is a curious encounter for everyone. The Samburu share the

DAVID ELSE | LPI

customs of the Maasai – including a culture centred around their livestock, and a penchant for exquisitely colourful beadwork.

This trek blends the Samburu/Ndorobo and European history of Kenya. The rugged mountains are inaccessible to motorised transport and the pencil cedar and podocarpus forests remain pristine. It's a taste of old Africa in one of East Africa's last true wildernesses.

RESPONSIBLE TRAVEL CREDENTIALS

- **The trails are ancient routes followed by animals and tribespeople. Low-impact camps are set up each evening.**

- **Peter Faull, his wife, Rosalie, and their UK office team established the Leroghi Mountains Conservation Fund in 2002, which has developed a series of simple, community-based projects aimed at educating school children in traditions of forest management and land care. It also provides funding for better fencing for reforestation and livestock protection for locals.**

- **A proportion of revenue from each client is directed towards these projects.**

WHEN TO GO

The Classic El Bogoi Route trek operates year-round. Tropical temperatures are tempered by the altitude (trekking at 1800m to 2400m). Daytime temperatures range between 20°C and 25°C and fall at night to 12°C to 15°C.

GETTING THERE

Samburu Treks is headed up by Peter and Rosalie Faull. Peter leads the treks, while Rosalie is head chef and botanist. The trek is supported by a team of pack-donkeys – the traditional mode of transport in the mountains.

The six-day Classic El Bogoi Route is suitable for anyone of moderate fitness. Longer, shorter and more challenging treks are also available.

Camp sites are comfortable but not luxurious – this is wilderness camping, where everything has to be carried. But there are hot bucket showers and gourmet meals featuring local game and produce.

The tour costs from US$1060 per person, twin share, including all meals, fees, guide services and transport. The trek starts near Maralal in northern Kenya. Road or air transfers can be arranged from Nairobi.

FACING PAGE: The semi-nomadic Samburu people to the north of Mt Kenya still lead traditional pastoral lifestyles, dressing in distinctive red cloth and handcrafted beadwork.

Further information: www.samburutrails.com

MADAGASCAR ~ RANOMAFANA NATIONAL PARK: LEAPING LEMURS

BY KERRY LORIMER

A mong the Milne-Edwards sifakas (a species of lemur) of Madagascar, chicks rule: matriarchs have the say-so on sifaka social life. Sadly, female dominance is a rare thing among mammals. Sadder still is that there are less than 5000 of these primitive primates left – and that number appears to be shrinking.

Madagascar is an ecological ark where lemurs – primates found nowhere else on earth – come in 51 varieties. But at the current rate of deforestation, many scientists predict there won't be any lemurs left in 20 years.

Dr Patricia Wright has been studying the sifakas of Ranomafana National Park for 18 years. She's discovered a new lemur species, set up community conservation projects and been awarded a knighthood by the Madagascar government. Four times a year she gets groups of paying Earthwatch volunteers to lend a hand.

With some preliminary instruction, volunteers spend their days following Milne-Edwards sifakas as they travel through the forest, noting behavioural data that will hopefully help unscramble the code to the lemurs' survival.

The park's tenants include 13 species of lemur, from the bug-eyed aye aye to the red-bellied, the black-and-white-ruffed, and the sportive lemurs. But the sifakas are the show ponies, making gasp-inducing leaps through the forest canopy with effortless grace. They're also less shy than their cousins, and often come down from the trees – the whole family group within metres of human observers – to feed and frolic on the forest floor.

Lacking lemurs' leaping ability, humans struggle a bit to keep up – the sifakas lead ground-bound volunteers on a dance through dense forest, often over steep and slippery terrain. It can also be wet and cold, but if you were ever inspired by Gerald Durrell's tales of this African ark, the chance to spend two weeks (rather than a momentary glimpse) with some of the world's most rare and charming creatures is well worth the effort.

ZED NELSON | EARTHWATCH

RESPONSIBLE TRAVEL CREDENTIALS

- **This is the first and longest study of a Malagasy primate. As deforestation encroaches on their geographically limited habitat, the results of the study will inform conservation strategies for all lemur species.**

- **Volunteer teams have played a major role in understanding the sifaka population – the current Plan of Management for the park is based in part on data collected by the project's past volunteers.**

- **Earthwatch is a not-for-profit organisation – participation fees help fund the ongoing project.**

WHEN TO GO

The projects usually run in June/July and November/December.

GETTING THERE

Air Mauritius flies to Antananarivo (Tana), Madagascar's capital.

The Earthwatch Madagascar's Lemurs project rendezvous is in Fianarantsoa (Fianar), which can be reached by direct Air Madagascar flight from Antananarivo. Or you can hire a car from one of the rental agencies located in the city centre.

The 15-day project costs US$2395 per person, including all meals and training. You'll be staying at the Centre ValBio research station – you need your own tent, but there are hot showers, flush toilets and good French- and Malagasy-inspired food.

You will be following a group of sifakas from dawn to dusk for five consecutive days each week. There will also be time for visiting local villages and relaxing in the park's hot mineral spring pool.

Be prepared for mud, a few insects (and leeches) and some tough hiking.

Further information: www.earthwatch.org

MALI ~ DOGON COUNTRY: ANCIENT DWELLINGS DOT A WRINKLED ESCARPMENT

BY ABIGAIL HOLE

I slept wrapped in the starlit night on the rooftop of a mud-built house, floating above a sea of darkness. Woken by the slow light of the morning; all around me were the smells and sounds of the village stirring: woodsmoke and children's chatter. It was the first morning of my trek from village to village in Dogon Country, one of West Africa's most famous and mysterious regions.

On the trail my guide, Boubacar, ran through the traditional Dogon greetings whenever he passed an acquaintance. The greetings lilted like music.

O se-wa-ma? (How are you?) – *Se-wa.* (I'm well.) – *O mara se-wa ma?* (How's your family?) – *Se-wa.* (They're well.)

The stream of inquiries to check the health of the person's father, mother, children and so on continued long after they had passed each other.

It's an otherworldly formality for an otherworldly place. Here the dwellings of the Dogon people are clustered around a 150km-long, sheer, burnished-red, wrinkled escarpment. The villages look like scattered rocks against the landscape's barren heat, dotted by surprised-looking baobab trees and improbable small, neat fields. Villages have distinctive architecture – granaries with witches-hat roofs, and protective animist fetishes, usually phallic mounds of mud, covered in porridge. The ancient dwellings of a former tribe, the Tellem, pock the escarpment and provoke legends about how on earth they were able to reach them.

You can trek in the Dogon for anything up to three weeks. It's remote and magical, but not undiscovered, which is why it's so important to choose your guide, route and type of trip carefully to minimise your impact on the region and get the most out of your trip.

DAVID ELSE LPI

RESPONSIBLE TRAVEL CREDENTIALS

- **To take off-the-beaten-track routes and learn Dogon etiquette, use local services and guides, or companies that employ people locally and give something back. By learning about the local culture you'll minimise the impact of your travel on this sensitive region. I booked my guide through Toguna Adventure Tours, run by a Dogon-American couple, and my flight through Point Afrique, the cooperative charter airline. Both provide training for local guides.**

- **Point Afrique runs charter flights into the region and guided tours. It reinvests its profits in the regions it visits, operates flights to encourage tourism in deprived areas and provides a microcredit scheme for local tourism workers.**

WHEN TO GO

November to February is the best season to trek. It's fiercely hot from March to May but you could still walk early in the morning. June to September is the rainy season, but downpours are short, the air is clear and flowers are spectacular.

GETTING THERE

Point Afrique flies from France to Bamako or Mopti in Mali.

From Bamako travel to Mopti via car or bus, from where you can take transport to one of the gateway towns, either Bandiagara or Bankass.

Whoever you go with, do some research and help plan your own route. The trekking is gentle – around three hours' walking in the morning, a four-hour break in a village to have lunch and wait for the heat of the day to subside and then three hours' walking in the afternoon.

Guide fees, including food, accommodation, transfer to and from gateway towns and village fees, are around US$20 to US$40 per day.

How to Tell if your Holiday is Green or Just Greenwash

You want to book an ecofriendly holiday, but so many travel brochures literally gloss over those thorny issues of environmental impact and 'giving something back'... How do you tell the difference between the good guys and the greenwash? Here area a few tips on choosing a tour operator or ecofriendly accommodation.

TIP NUMBER ONE

Tour operators, hotels and lodges that are genuine in their approach to responsible tourism will generally have a written policy covering their environmental impact, employment and cultural policy. Usually it will be posted on their website, but they should be able to show it to you in some written form. If they don't, ask them why – by their response, you'll be able to make a judgement call.

TIP NUMBER TWO

Ask some specifics about how operators implement their policy:

- What do they see are the key environmental issues facing them and how are they dealing with them? For example, how does their recycling work? How do they minimise the impact of their tours on walking trails and villages and wilderness areas? How do they avoid overcrowding?

- Do they employ local guides and leaders? Many international tour operators still primarily use Western leaders. In some countries, such as Thailand, this is actually illegal. While there are situations where a Westerner's expertise can't be sourced locally, in most cases, you'll get a far better insight into the places you're visiting if you're shown around by someone who was born there and knows it like the back of their hand.

- What training opportunities do they provide for their staff, at all levels? Are guides trained in responsible tourism practices, eg approaching wildlife and camp-site etiquette? Are they able to interpret the landscape and culture effectively for their clients?

- What additional information on environmental and cultural sensitivities and other educational information is provided to clients?

- Does the company limit the size of its groups to minimise impact and maximise interaction with the host community?

- Has the company been invited to visit the villages, or build the hotel by the local people themselves? Are the locals happy to have them there?

- Do they have a 'green' purchasing policy? What proportion of their produce, building materials, services etc are sourced from the immediate local area? What is their fair trade policy?

- What sort of accommodation do they use? Is it family-owned and how environmentally sustainable is it? For example, many trekking lodges are still burning forests to provide food and hot showers for tourists. Kerosene and solar power are alternative energy sources.

- What proportion of revenue remains in, or reverts to the local community? (On a lot of 'all-inclusive' packages, the answer is 'very little'.)

- Do they work with any local charities or conservation projects, or have they initiated any projects of their own? What are they doing to 'give back to the community'?

TIP NUMBER THREE

In the immortal words of Kermit the frog: 'it's not [always] easy being green'. So if an operator is getting it right, they'll be proud of it. Ask them what their biggest successes have been: a project started, a milestone met.

From the true believers – the best practitioners – you'll hear heart-warming stories of philanthropy, partnerships, pride and passion. And the best thing is, these principles infuse all aspects of the travel service they provide – and that means your experience, too.

FACING PAGE: Local operators can give you unique insights into a culture, but ask a few questions to be sure the 'minority' people you're visiting are happy to have you there.

MOROCCO ~ KASBAH DU TOUBKAL: A LUXURIOUS TASTE OF TRADITIONAL BERBER HOSPITALITY

BY KERRY LORIMER

The Kasbah du Toubkal rose from the ruins of a 1940s summerhouse, owned by a member of the local ruling family. It's now a luxury boutique hotel and conference centre, renowned as having some of the best views in North Africa. The rooms are unabashedly luxurious – and the food rates with the best in Morocco. You can sip mint tea on a rooftop terrace and soak in the views of Jebl Toubkal, North Africa's highest mountain, or soak in the steamy decadence of the *hammam* (traditional steam bathhouse).

Following Morocco's independence in 1956, the Kasbah, a rose-coloured fortress overlooking the village of Imlil and shadowed by the snowy peaks of the Atlas Mountains, was abandoned to crumble away along with others of its ilk. Its restoration began in 1990, when UK-owned travel company Discover Ltd, which had been operating in Morocco for 20 years, purchased the decrepit shell.

The construction project was a joint venture with the Berber people of the Imlil valley. It used local labour and traditional methods wherever possible – not that there was a choice, since access was by mule and electricity didn't arrive until 1997. It's now run by staff from the surrounding villages, who bring the experience of traditional Berber hospitality to their guests.

The architectural lines are faithful to tradition – but with a little window dressing, the Kasbah also stood in as a Tibetan monastery in *Kundun*, Martin Scorsese's 1997 film about the Dalai Lama.

The Kasbah is a destination in itself, but it's also a great base for exploring the Atlas Mountains and Toubkal National Park. The hotel can arrange treks of varying lengths, including climbs of Jebl Toubkal, after which a steam and soak in the *hammam* is mandatory.

ALAN KEOHANE

RESPONSIBLE TRAVEL CREDENTIALS

- Funding from the Kasbah has supported a rubbish management system and environmentally appropriate incinerators for surrounding villages.

- The Kasbah was developed in part to extend the tradition of Berber hospitality, which it does through employing hotel staff, guides, porters and other tradespeople from the Ait Mizane tribe in the surrounding valley.

- Discover Ltd directly financed the purchase of an ambulance for Imlil. Five per cent of the Kasbah's income as well as donations from visitors go towards the running costs of the ambulance and to a village association, which uses the money to fund community projects.

WHEN TO GO

The heat of the high season (June to September) is tempered by the Kasbah's 1800m elevation, but consequently it's heavily booked in this period. Winter means snow and serious cold – ice climbing is an option on Jebl Toubkal.

GETTING THERE

The Kasbah is 60km and 90 minutes from Marrakech. You can reach it by taxi or hire car, followed by a 15-minute walk or mule ride from Imlil.

There is overnight accommodation for 22, ranging from en suite bedrooms to a self-contained private house. Prices range from €30 to €200 per person, per night. Conference facilities cater for 60.

MOZAMBIQUE ~ NKWICHI LODGE:
STAR GAZING ON LAKE NYASA

BY KERRY LORIMER

COURTESY OF MANDA WILDERNESS PROJECT

Lake Malawi (Lake Nyasa in Mozambique) comes as a surprise to first-timers. It's the third-biggest lake in Africa (560km long) and has more garishly-hued fish (1000 species) swimming around in its gin-clear fresh water than any other inland body of water on earth. It's fringed by sandy beaches, flanked by forest and divides Malawi from Mozambique.

Mozambique is recovering after 40 years of civil war and, in Lake Nyasa's most gorgeous corner, the Manda Wilderness project has assumed a prominent role in the country's tourism renaissance.

Nkwichi Lodge was built with local labour from sustainable local materials in a faintly Flintstone-esque style, with boulders and branches protruding into rooms and four-posters fashioned from chunky logs. Which is not to say it lacks elegance or comfort: there are just seven secluded, crisp-sheeted chalets, each with its own outdoor en suite, where you shower under the stars or with a view of the lake.

Down by the lake shore, the sand is super-fine and the water inviting: you can snorkel, sail, paddle a canoe or simply swing in a hammock. The Nyanja people who helped build and now staff the lodge warmly encourage you to visit their villages or offer to guide you on a walk next door through the Manda Game Reserve for a bit of bird-watching and game-spotting.

With guidance and assistance from the Manda Wilderness Community Trust, established by Nkwichi's founders, 14 local villages have set up the 100,000-hectare community-owned reserve, where wildlife populations decimated during the wars are now reviving.

The Community Trust has also funded schools and medical facilities and guests are encouraged to visit the Manda Horticultural Project on the neighbouring farm, where farmers have learned to grow a variety of fresh produce: the resulting fruit and veg supplies Nkwichi's restaurant.

You could easily spend four or five days at Nkwichi – it's supremely relaxing and the hospitality's delightful – and it would be a fine way to cap off a safari holiday.

RESPONSIBLE TRAVEL CREDENTIALS

- **To encourage the return of big game to the Manda Wilderness Community Game Reserve, the communities involved in setting up and managing the reserve have agreed to stop cutting and burning the forest and hunting with snares and dogs. The reserve habitat is showing healthy signs of recovery.**

- **The Manda Horticultural Project now involves eight villages and aims to improve nutrition through better agricultural practices. So far, over 350 farmers have received assistance and a new market has been set up in nearby Cobue.**

- **The Manda Community Trust has funded the building of schools, medical facilities and other public works. Villagers vote on priorities and the Trust provides financial support in return for the villagers providing the labour.**

- **Nkwichi is the biggest local employer and provides training in tourism. The lodge owners claim that staying at the lodge provides wages for up to 50 local members of staff, who in turn each support up to 15 members of their direct families. That adds up to your stay impacting on the lives of 750 people.**

- **For every visitor, every night, the lodge contributes US$5 towards the Community Trust.**

WHEN TO GO

The dry season lasts from late April to October or November and is the best time to visit.

GETTING THERE

There is no direct road access to the lodge: you must travel the last stage by boat. It is accessible by charter flight, yacht or the historic *Illala* ferry from the Malawian side, or by scheduled flight from Maputo to Lichinga, plus a four-hour drive from the Mozambique side. Any of the above methods will bring you to a point from where the lodge's motorboat will collect you. (See the website for more detailed information.)

Nkwichi Lodge takes up to 14 guests. Prices start at around US$160 per person, twin share, including all meals and non-motorised activities.

NAMIBIA ~ DAMARALAND CAMP:
A BLUEPRINT UNION OF
COMMUNITY & CONSERVATION

BY KERRY LORIMER

DANA ALLEN | WILDERNESS SAFARIS

DANA ALLEN / WILDERNESS SAFARIS

Y̲ou won't see vast hordes of migrating wildebeest or encounter many members of the Big Five when you stay at Damaraland Camp in Namibia. Rather, the fascination is in the detail – and in the stark, humbling stillness of the desert.

Located 90km inland from Torra Bay on Namibia's Skeleton Coast, Damaraland is the country's – and one of Africa's – most successful community tourism ventures.

Until a decade ago, the local wildlife was diminishing at a rapid rate and virtually no-one in the local community had a job. Safari camp operator Wilderness Safaris joined forces with the local Riemvasmaker people and a number of concerned aid and conservation organisations to establish Damaraland Camp as a blueprint for community tourism projects. Around 350,000 hectares are now under protection, wildlife numbers are thriving and the local people have training, income and are actively engaged in land and wildlife management.

Ten luxury tents squat rather insignificantly amid a landscape of vast views and enormous plains edging up to huge mountains. Morning mists creep inland from the coast, providing just enough moisture to sustain well-adapted desert life.

Most famous of the local inhabitants is the rare desert elephant, which is smaller than its more generic brethren and able to regularly stroll 70km between drinks.

Daily camp routine usually involves game drives and nature walks where the Damaraland guides breathe life into the arid landscape, explaining the intricate adaptations of desert dwellers, from the tiniest insect to the black rhinoceros, oryx, kudu and other species that have made a tenuous contract with life in the desert.

There are also visits to the famous Twyfelfontein Bushman engravings and you can borrow a mountain bike to explore or just lie back and gaze into an inky, uninterrupted desert sky.

RESPONSIBLE TRAVEL CREDENTIALS

- **Many of the animal populations have doubled since 1996, since the project was established. Both animals and endemic arid-zone plants are now under conservancy protection.**

- **Damaraland Camp won the overall 2005 Tourism for Tomorrow Conservation award.**

- **The camp is staffed by people from the local community – training and mentoring is provided.**

- **Inspired by the success of Damaraland, the neighbouring Doro Nawas community has established its own 400,000-hectare conservancy.**

- **Ten per cent of room revenues are returned to the community and have been used to fund the local school, stock loss compensation programmes and other uplift projects.**

- **Where wildlife was once seen as a threat, it's now regarded as an important economic asset.**

WHEN TO GO

The rainy season is from November to April, and it's also very hot at this time. From May to August nights can be very cold, but days pleasant, up to about 30°C. Best game viewing is from about June to October.

GETTING THERE

There are 10 large, comfortable permanent tents, all with en suite, veranda and valley views. Each also has a flush toilet and hot shower. There is a separate communal living area with a rock pool.

Activities include four-wheel-drive and walking safaris, and mountain bikes are available.

Prices start at US$332 per person, twin share, fully inclusive.

Damaraland Camp is accessible by two-wheel-drive vehicle (as far as the car park), off the C39 from Windhoek about 110km before Torra Bay. There is also an airstrip under construction 14km from the camp; staff will collect you on arrival. You can link with other Wilderness Safaris camps in southern Africa.

FACING PAGE: Damaraland's nomadic, desert-adapted elephants have increased in number from around 50 to 600 animals over the past 20 years. Their range has also extended and now impacts on local people. Community-led conservation efforts are seen as the elephants' best chance for survival.

Further information: www.wilderness-safaris.com but you need to book via a travel agent

NAMIBIA ~ KALAHARI DESERT:
LEARNING HOW NOT TO STARVE IN THE SAND
BY KERRY LORIMER

ARIADNE VAN ZANDBERGEN LPI

The San Bushmen have survived and thrived in one of the harshest environments on earth – the Kalahari Desert – for at least 40,000 years. They're one of the oldest surviving peoples on earth and one of the very few who can exist without a permanent above-ground water source.

So they can teach a city-slicker a thing or two about staying alive in the wilderness.

Heading out on a hunt with a small band of San, the men will carry bows and arrows, digging sticks and little else. They manage to move virtually silently through the landscape, reading its language and responding so skilfully, the clumsy foreigner stumbling in their wake is usually left feeling both awed and inadequate (much to the amusement of the hunters!).

On a morning's outing, you might get to try the 'fruits' of the desert (berries and tubers – the San have names for over 300 plants), or – if you're really lucky – to watch the finely-honed procedure for stalking larger game such as antelope. With the simplest of weapons, combined with consummate skill and teamwork, the San are able to bring down even a kudu (large antelope) with their poison-tipped arrows.

There are no contrived or scheduled 'interactions' with the San when you stay at Tsumkwe Lodge, where the proprietors, Arno and Estelle Oosthuysen, aim to give you a sensitive introduction to the people of the nearby Ju/'hoansi villages and their way of life.

From the lodge, they can arrange a translator to take you to visit nearby Ju/'hoan villages, but for a better understanding, it's worth staying a night or two in the small bush camp beside the village of //Nhoq'ma. In a joint venture with the villagers, the Oosthuysens use the camp as a base for unstructured, guided cultural tours. When you go out with the //Nhoq'ma hunters, it's to wherever the hunters want to go that day or where they've found something promising, such as a possible honey nest or fresh porcupine tracks. At some point during your stay, you'll witness a traditional healing dance, performed to entertain both guests and community, as well as to cure the sick.

By camping by the village and getting involved in 'daily life', visitors and San have a chance to get to know each other as individuals – instead of just as members of a different 'culture'.

RESPONSIBLE TRAVEL CREDENTIALS

- **Tsumkwe Lodge makes direct payments to the villagers, part of which is a flat day rate, and also a payment per overnight visitor. The //Nhoq'ma villagers earn around US$12,300 per year from their involvement with Tsumkwe. As a result, the standard of clothing and nutrition has increased since the partnership was formed, and all the village children now attend school. The Oosthuysens also assist with school transport and uniforms.**

- **The building materials for the tented camp were purchased from the villagers and, although the Oosthuysens built the camp, the villagers own it.**

WHEN TO GO

The rainy season is from November to April, and it's also very hot at this time. From May to August nights can be very cold, but days pleasant, up to about 30°C. Best game viewing is from about June to October.

GETTING THERE

Tsumkwe Lodge lies at the heart of, but is not part of, the Nyae Nyae conservancy. It's in Namibia's northern Kalahari, about 500km of tar road plus 200km of gravel road from Windhoek. It's accessible by two-wheel drive car or (very costly) charter flight. There are nine rooms in total, each with en suite bathroom and solar lighting – simple but comfortable. Staying here costs US$280 per night, twin share, including all meals.

The tented camp next to the village has four twin-bedded tents, separate long-drop loos and bucket showers – no frills. A guide will stay here with you, and this costs the same, but includes the tour activities.

Visitors to Tsumkwe Lodge who don't book the //Nhoq'ma visit can visit other villages in the Nyae Nyae area with a Ju/'hoan-English translator, which the Tsumkwe staff can arrange. They must use their own (four-wheel drive) vehicle and pay about US$82 per group for a four-hour bushwalk.

Further information: Expert Africa in the UK works closely with the Tsumkwe Lodge and can advise on its suitability for your interests – www.expertafrica.com

RWANDA & UGANDA ~ BWINDI IMPENETRABLE NATIONAL PARK: LINGUISTIC ENCOUNTERS WITH THE SONS OF KING KONG

BY KERRY LORIMER

RICHARD FIELD & REBECCA FRASER

As with any cross-cultural encounter, it pays to speak some basic gorilla when you come face to face with a silverback. Chances are he'll waste no time showing you who's boss: chest thumping and mock charges are customary overtures. The appropriate response involves clearing your throat and generally acting like a wimp, which is gorilla for 'whatever you say, sir'.

But once the pecking order is established, family life in the jungle returns pretty much to normal and the small band of humans crouching among the foliage gets a privileged peek into the lives and loves of some of our closest relatives.

Mothers suckle and groom newborns as older apes rumble, squabble and shriek much like adolescents anywhere. Having proved his point, the silverback feigns utter disinterest, effortlessly shredding small trees with canines the size of popsicles, and occasionally swatting a youngster who's showing insufficient respect for its elders.

It's eerily like watching a television sitcom – but far more riveting, and possibly more 'human'.

Sharing an hour with gorillas in the wild is a privilege that requires some effort. It can take you and your machete-wielding guide most of a morning to track a family to its 'playground'. It's steep and steamy – but utterly unforgettable.

There are just 650 mountain gorillas left in the wild, all located in the equatorial mountains of Uganda, Rwanda and the Democratic Republic of Congo. Currently, tourism is confined to Rwanda and Uganda and is strictly limited: each habituated gorilla group can receive just a single one-hour visit per day, group sizes are capped, and each visitor must have a prepurchased permit costing US$375. A hefty price? Not when you consider the revenue raised has essentially ensured the gorillas' survival to date: to local governments, gorillas are a valuable commodity. Consequently, large tracts of habitat have been protected and antipoaching campaigns established.

Approach distances are strictly controlled to minimise impact on the 'natural' behaviour of the apes and to prevent transmission of human diseases.

Gorilla researcher and conservationist Dian Fossey had doubts the great apes would survive the 20th century. Sustainable tourism may just ensure we can speak face-to-face gorilla in another hundred years.

RESPONSIBLE TRAVEL CREDENTIALS

- **As a result of tourism, more reserves and conservation and education programmes are being implemented in the region.**

- **It's estimated that each habituated gorilla earns its country around US$90,000 per annum in direct park revenue – and probably 10 times that in indirect revenue. Additionally, these funds go towards establishing and maintaining other parks in the country.**

- **Local people are employed as trackers and wardens providing services to tourists. However, only US$20 per person from park entry fees goes towards community conservation projects.**

WHEN TO GO

It's possible to get gorilla permits year-round. Be prepared for rain and muddy going at any time of the year. The wettest period is generally from October to December and then April and May.

GETTING THERE

Bwindi Impenetrable National Park in Uganda is currently Africa's most popular gorilla-tracking destination and sightings are almost guaranteed. Mgahinga National Park has less certainty while Rwanda's Parc Nacionale des Volcans also offers guarantees. You must have a gorilla-tracking permit, purchased either through a tour operator or from the park office.

Most African tour operators offer gorilla treks and you can also do it independently – however, tour companies make block bookings and it's first in, best dressed for the leftover permits (available at the park entry office).

UK-based Discovery Initiatives has developed its itineraries in conjunction with the International Gorilla Conservation Project (IGCP) and Dian Fossey Gorilla Fund International, which allow access to their experts and visits to community projects. The company makes a US$100 per person contribution to these NGOs' community conservation and research efforts. Each tour is led by a recognised primatologist and allows visitors to get a better understanding of the issues that local people and wildlife face in this region.

Discovery Initiatives' 14-day Mountain Gorilla 'Conservation in Action' Safari costs from £3495 departing London, or £3195 departing Entebbe, Uganda, and includes permits to visit three separate gorilla families in Uganda and Rwanda. Departures are in January and September.

SOUTH AFRICA ~ CAPE TOWN:
EXPERIENCE TOWNSHIP LIFE WITH THE LOCALS

BY SIMON RICHMOND

ERIC L WHEATER LPI

The main tourist season is from December to March (when it's the hottest). Other times of year are just as good times to visit.

GETTING THERE

Cape Town has direct international flights with Europe, Asia and the Americas.

Half-day tours cost around US$38 to US$45.

Overnight accommodation with breakfast for single/double starts at US$25/50.

Generally rife with poverty, AIDS, drug taking and crime, South African townships, such as Khayelitsha in Cape Town, are hardly your average holiday destination. Nevertheless township tours have become one of the most popular activities on the Cape with scores of operators running bus trips around the townships of Langa, Guguletu, Crossroads and Khayelitsha – home to an estimated 1.8 million black Capetonians. The success of such tours, which run the risk of being voyeuristic, are down to residents and their desire to show that township life in the new South Africa is far more positive, hopeful and vibrant than many would expect.

Most tours follow similar itineraries, starting at the excellent District Six Museum in the city centre to learn about the apartheid system and how it came to destroy areas such as District Six where all races lived side by side. From the museum the tours head east to the townships. Among the sights visited are the Guga S'Thebe arts and cultural centre in Langa; the Philani Nutrition Centre in Crossroads, which runs a weaving factory and a printing operation; and Rosie's Soup Kitchen, where the saintly Rosie has been serving some 600 meals a day to the poor for years.

One of the most popular stops is Vicky's B&B in Khayelitsha, home of the irrepressible Vicky Ntozini. In the late 1990s Vicky was one of the first to turn her home, which like many others in the township is built of scrap, into a guesthouse. Mother to four children and wife to mechanic Picksteel, Vicky is typical of the determined, jovial Xhosa women who have kept communities such as Khayelitsha going through good times and bad. Her home has that luxury in the townships – an internal shower and toilet, a gift to Vicky from a local hotel chain. For dinner you'll be treated to traditional African dishes such as *samp* (thick maize porridge) or even a 'smily' – a grinning sheep's head, stewed then caramelised by blowtorch!

If you're looking for a bit more luxury, try Thope Lekau's Kopanong in the most affluent part of Khayelitsha, where the reasonably large brick-built homes are practically palaces compared to shacks such as Vicky's. Run by the dynamic Lekau, who's a registered guide and experienced development worker, this place has had diplomats and overseas politicians as guests. Like many others they have found that bedding down in Khayelitsha is the best way to experience the warm and generous hospitality that black South Africans call *ubuntu*.

RESPONSIBLE TRAVEL CREDENTIALS

- **Some operators are better than others at channelling funds back into the community. Grassroutes and Daytrippers, for example, are both involved in the Tourism Community Development Trust (www.tcdtrust.org.za), which has helped build a crèche in the townships.**

- **To ensure your money helps those in the townships stay overnight in one of the growing band of B&Bs or arrange a meal at one of several restaurants that are based there. Also buy locally made souvenirs: if you're in Khayelitsha on Monday or Thursday the craft market at St Michael's Church is a great place to shop.**

Further information: kopanong@xsinet.co.za | www.journey.digitalspace.net/vicky.html www.grassroutetours.co.za | www.daytrippers.co.za

SOUTH AFRICA ~ DE WILDT CHEETAH & WILDLIFE CENTRE:
BEHIND THE SCENES WITH WARP-DRIVE WONDERS

BY JAMES JEFFREY

Y ou can go like the wind, you can go like the clappers – but it's a fair bet you'll never go like the cheetah. At full belt, the world's fastest land animal combines sinuous muscularity with balletic flexibility and ballistic velocity as it zeros in on the nearest impala. But all the nature documentary footage in the world can never prepare you for the wonder of seeing a cheetah in the flesh as it launches into warp drive, exploding from 0km to 100km in less time than a Lamborghini and streaking into the distance like an artillery shell in a fur coat.

Watching the big cats run at the De Wildt Cheetah and Wildlife Centre is just one of many exhilarating moments on the Wildlife – Behind the Scenes tour. Situated just up the road from Pretoria, De Wildt grew out of the obsession of cheetah devotee Ann van Dyk and is one of the last obstacles blocking the creature's slide toward extinction. And it's not just cheetahs; De Wildt and its crew are doing their bit to save a whole ark of other species – including wild dogs, honey badgers, brown hyenas and Cape vultures – through a programme of breeding and, just as importantly, rigorous public education for everyone from wide-eyed school children to trigger-happy farmers.

Escorted by a wildlife veterinarian, the Behind the Scenes tour provides a glimpse beyond the enclosures and the convoys of tourist-laden safari vehicles and gives you privileged access to the inner circle, to the vets, the scientists and the researchers. And you won't just be a spectator; this is the chance to get some hands-on experience, from holding down vultures that look almost as big as garage doors while their wings are tagged, to carrying freshly tranquilised cheetahs from their enclosures into the veterinary clinic. (For such a phenomenal hunter, they feel surprisingly light and delicate.)

From De Wildt, the tour travels to an elephant sanctuary, then to Edeni, a privately owned wildlife reserve in the northeast of the country. Edeni sits right next door to the Kruger National Park, but lacks its famous neighbour's traffic levels, so the animals are more relaxed. As at De Wildt, you are in the hands of scientists and researchers at Edeni and the days are spent radio tracking cheetahs and lions; giving elephants a respectful berth; counting warthogs, rhinos and hornbills; listening to the barking of baboons; and watching the sun sink among the mountains beyond the acacia-studded plain.

RESPONSIBLE TRAVEL CREDENTIALS

- **Extinction is a very real and present danger for cheetahs and wild dogs, as well as a range of other species encountered on this tour. They need all the help they can get. Some of the most important work to ensure their continued survival is being done here.**

- **Local guides and wildlife experts extend your comprehension beyond the purely scientific or ecological and help you to understand how everything fits together in the African cultural and natural universe.**

- **A portion of your fare goes directly to the De Wildt Cheetah and Wildlife Centre, enabling it to continue its work: it gets no government funding.**

- **Your presence and your wallet also help provide employment – from house and kitchen staff to rangers and security – in a country plagued by stratospheric unemployment levels.**

WHEN TO GO

The tour runs all year-round.

GETTING THERE

The Wildlife – Behind the Scenes tour, operated by Peregrine in conjunction with De Wildt, starts and ends in Johannesburg.

The tour lasts eight days and costs US$5870 per person, twin share, land content only.

De Wildt Cheetah and Wildlife Centre is approximately an hour's drive from Pretoria. Edeni is five hours' drive, or a short flight to the local airport at Hoedspruit.

FACING PAGE: Cheetahs can reach their top speed of over 100km/h in about three seconds and are the only cats that can change direction, mid-air, at speed.

TANZANIA ~ CHUMBE ISLAND CORAL PARK:
COCONUTS, CRABS, CORAL & CONSERVATION
BY RICHARD FIELD

RICHARD FIELD & REBECCA FRASER

RICHARD FIELD & REBECCA FRASER

Hamise, the senior guide at Chumbe Island Coral Park, held in his hand the biggest damn crab I had ever seen. It was a coconut crab (aka a robber crab). Being large, slow and easy to catch, they have become extinct in most areas where they co-exist with humans. At last report, only three islands in the Indian Ocean had any coconut crabs at all, with Chumbe Island having by far the healthiest population.

'Watch the power of its pincers', Hamise said, as the crab went about obliterating a hapless lead pencil, with no discernible effort. Photographs were taken, after which Hamise, 10 fingers still intact, returned the crab to the forest, and we returned to our dinner.

Coconut crabs are definitely important members of Chumbe's terrestrial ecosystem, but they are only a small part of what makes this island special. Chumbe is a privately managed nature reserve that originated from the need to protect the island's reef, widely acclaimed to have one of the world's best coral gardens. Along with the corals and a myriad of reef fish, the guided snorkelling excursions normally encounter turtles and dolphins and many other creatures that would generally go unnoticed without the eagle-eyed guides!

Ninety per cent of the island consists of the only remaining pristine coral rag forest in Zanzibar. The forest is now home to a breeding programme for Ader's duiker, one of the world's most endangered antelopes.

All the conservation projects are funded by the island's responsible tourism enterprise. Visitors can overnight in the delightfully romantic eco-villa, built in traditional Swahili style using materials from local suppliers. Rainfall is stored in huge holding tanks underneath each unit, and is then pumped to a tank on the roof where it is solar heated for showers. Lighting comes from solar power, grey water is filtered and used for irrigation, and the toilets are of the non-smelly compost variety.

All this really means is guilt-free afternoon siestas, either on the beach or in your own private hammock!

RESPONSIBLE TRAVEL CREDENTIALS

- **Each building on the island is completely self-sustaining with virtually no impact on the environment. The coral park has successfully managed to protect a pristine coral island ecosystem in an area that is otherwise heavily over-fished and over-exploited. All activities have a strong emphasis on education and conservation.**

- **Chumbe is staffed and managed by local people from nearby fishing villages on Zanzibar. They are able to pass on their knowledge about conservation to the other villagers. The lodge funds an education programme where children from schools on Zanzibar are brought to the island to spend a day learning about coral reefs and the need for their conservation.**

- **Profits from the lodge are reinvested directly into the island's education, conservation and research programmes.**

WHEN TO GO

June through to August are the busiest times, but also the coolest months. September through to December are reputed to be the best months, with warm, clear water and low-season rates.

GETTING THERE

Chumbe is located just off Zanzibar's west coast, about 8km southwest of Stonetown. It can be reached by a 30- to 45-minute boat ride from the Mbweni Ruins Hotel (about 15 minutes' drive south of Stonetown). Daily departures are at 10am.

Accommodation consists of seven luxury, en suite 'eco-bandas'. Rates vary from US$150 to US$200 per person per night depending on the season.

Boat transfers, meals, soft drinks and guided activities are included in the price.

Further information: www.chumbeisland.com

ZAMBIA ~ ZAMBEZI RIVER:
HANGING OUT WITH HIPPOS
BY KERRY LORIMER

JOE MANN | LPI

As a three-tonne hippo crashes into the water at full speed (around 30km/h) or lets out a bellowing snort that seems to set your tent canvas shivering, it's hard to think of Africa's most dangerous beast as 'delicate'. Go figure: in one of the most punishing environments on earth, the hippo has evolved to be susceptible to sunburn.

The hippo's solar sensitivity is a canoeist's carte blanche to get up close and personal, in an unobtrusive way. Hippos spend most of their day beside, in or under water, protecting their pink and brown hide from the African sun. As you paddle a canoe down the mighty Zambezi River, which separates Zambia from Zimbabwe, hippos in their hundreds loaf on the banks like over-stuffed sofas; or trundle and splash into the gently eddying river; or lie submerged, with just a snout and bobble eyes above water.

For the most part, the hippos don't give a snort about being watched and get about their loafing and wallowing unperturbed. The same goes for the elephants, which seem to regard passing paddlers as moving wallpaper.

The stretch of the Zambezi from the Kariba Gorge to the confluence of the Chongwe River is stuffed with hippos, as well as elephants, crocodiles, impala, baboons and bountiful bird species. At first it's unsettling, to say the least, when a hippo surfaces just metres from your canoe, or when you find yourself looking *up* at an elephant, or when the midnight antics of a bull hippo sound as though he's about to trample your tent.

Holding the title of Africa's greatest man-killer (yes, more successful than lions, elephants or buffalo), hippos deserve respect – and negotiating routes around the numerous herds on the river requires the skills of an experienced guide. Your guide will introduce you to both the wildlife and the village life along the banks: small mud-hut villages dot the Zambian side and there are occasional stops for a chat and perhaps a bit of bartering for hand-crafted souvenirs.

Paddling the lazy pace of the Zambezi is like gliding through an interactive wildlife documentary – it's one of the best ways to be close to animals without disturbing them. You'll soon slip into the rhythm of Africa – and you may well be spoiled for any other way to watch wildlife.

RESPONSIBLE TRAVEL CREDENTIALS

- **Paddling a canoe and low-impact camping on river beaches makes negligible environmental impact, and is one of the least-intrusive ways of watching wildlife.**

- **Local guides and staff are employed, and souvenir-shopping in the villages sees money going direct to the locals.**

WHEN TO GO

The dry season, between July and October, is the best time.

GETTING THERE

A number of companies operate canoe trips on the Zambezi. UK-based Exodus offers eight-day trips including five days canoeing, game walks and a four-wheel-drive game drive, with camping at night on sandy river islands.

Canoes are large and stable two-person Canadian canoes that carry all the camping equipment and supplies. No previous experience necessary.

The Zambezi Valley trip costs £635 per person, twin share, excluding flights, departing from Lusaka in Zambia; all meals and equipment are included.

FACING PAGE: Not only are hippos susceptible to sunburn, they can't swim – or even float. Instead they have webbed feet and gallop in slow motion across the river bottom.

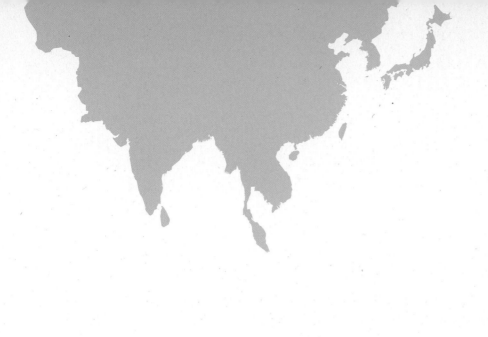

Asia

BHUTAN ~ PARO:
IS THIS SHANGRI-LA?
BY KERRY LORIMER

KERRY LORIMER

KERRY LORIMER

Sometimes Bhutan – the last Buddhist kingdom, high in the Himalaya – can appear too perfect. There are (visibly, at least) no beggars, forests still cover 70% of the country, no-one's starving or homeless and everyone loves the king.

On a three-day trek, we hiked through forest-flanked yak meadows where wisps of woodsmoke twirled from the chimneys of chalet-style shingled farmhouses. We followed trails through Tolkienesque primeval forests, where geriatric pine trees were carbuncled with mosses and festooned with old man's beard. And we emerged on high passes where pure breezes whisked the messages from strings of prayer flags.

The day before the famous Paro festival, held in the Paro Dzong (which is reminiscent of Lhasa's Potala Palace), we hiked up above the town and stumbled into a 'rehearsal'. I was greeted by a man dressed as a vaudevillian devil, who presented me with a large, red, wooden phallus – much to the hilarity of the locals. (Large, graphically depicted penises painted in pornographic pink are linked to Bhutanese mythology and appear on the walls of most dwellings.)

Young priests in elaborate masks and gorgeously gaudy costumes whirled like dervishes and performed improbable head-high leaps to the accompaniment of sonorous, farting horns and whooping cheers.

To the kids we were a curiosity (not once was I asked for a 'bonbon' or a pen), while their parents proudly offered interpretations of the dance and welcomed us into the picnic atmosphere.

In two weeks I never heard a bad word spoken about King Jigme Singye Wangchuck, despite his rather patriarchal approach to governing his people: among other things, he's decreed that everyone must wear traditional national costume and cigarette smoking is outlawed.

Sounds quaint? Well, it is, but King Wangchuck is also widely regarded as one of the most forward-thinking leaders in the region. Cut off by geography from the rest of the world, Bhutan didn't fully fling open its doors to the outside world until the mid-1970s. (Television arrived in 1999.)

Then the king had only to look to neighbouring Nepal to see what not to do in steering the development of his tiny nation. He has been guided by international advisors and, given the choice of two border-sharing evils, made the savvy decision to align the country with India, rather than China, which possibly offers a better guarantee that Bhutan's unique cultural integrity will be conserved.

Despite appearances, Bhutan isn't perfect, but its tourism industry is being incrementally developed, not solely to maximise economic return, but in reference to the measure of 'Gross National Happiness'. Culture and environment remain vibrantly 'intact' and tourist numbers are regulated – which makes for a tantalising travel destination.

RESPONSIBLE TRAVEL CREDENTIALS

- **Bhutan is often held up as the shining light of sustainable development and responsible tourism in Asia. By law at least 60% of the country's forests will remain intact in perpetuity.**

- **The country's development programme (in which tourism plays only a bit-part) balances the needs of community and cultural preservation (Gross National Happiness) against environmental conservation and economic expansion.**

- **In order to regulate tourist numbers and ensure tourist dollars remain in Bhutan, travellers must book all arrangements with a Bhutanese tour operator, the cost of which is covered by a US$200 per day visa fee. Around 35% of a visa fee goes to the government; the remainder goes to the Bhutanese tour operator.**

- **The high price of the visa is essentially aimed at discouraging budget travellers: lower numbers with fatter wallets are seen as the best option for tourism development. It's a delicate operation to manage – the government has welcomed international development partners, which are erecting luxury 'spas' at mildly alarming rates. But one wonders if the clientele of said establishments is the right 'fit' with Bhutan's desire to preserve its cultural and environmental integrity.**

WHEN TO GO

September to November is ideal: the major festivals occur during this time and the mountains are clearly visible on trek. March to May is also good. June to August is monsoon season and best avoided.

GETTING THERE

Druk Air is the only airline servicing Bhutan and has no interline arrangements with other international airlines, so you will need to book your connecting ticket separately. Druk will not issue a ticket without proof of a valid visa.

You must book – and pay for – your full itinerary with a Bhutanese tour operator before your visa will be issued. There is a range of quality Bhutanese operators. You can try booking direct, but adventure travel companies worldwide offer Bhutan tours and may be easier than dealing directly with Bhutan.

Visas cost US$200 per person per day, for the duration of your stay, which covers everything (unless you're staying at one of the exclusive new resorts whose tariffs exceed this price).

Further information: Yangphel Tours is one of Bhutan's leading tour operators – www.yangphel.com
Australia – www.peregrineadventures.com | UK – www.exodus.co.uk | USA – www.mtsobek.com

BORNEO ~ NANGA SUMPA:
A LIVING LONGHOUSE IN SARAWAK
BY KERRY LORIMER

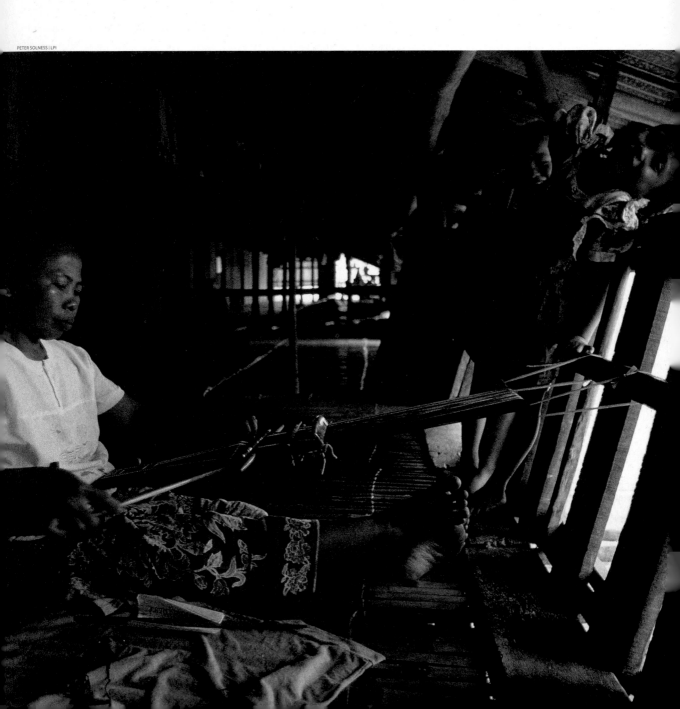

MARK DAFFEY / LPI

WHEN TO GO

It's tropically hot and sticky at any time, with monsoon rains falling (heavily, but intermittently) between November and February.

GETTING THERE

Nanga Sumpa is located in the Batang Ai region of Sarawak in Malaysian Borneo. Getting to Nanga Sampu is half the fun. After a four-hour bus trip from Kuching, you board outboard-powered longboats, cross the Batang Ai reservoir and then head upriver through breathtaking jungle, negotiating rapids and getting a taste of life on the river, to arrive several hours later at the longhouse.

A three-day trip, including two nights at Nanga Sumpa, with transfers from Kuching, guided walks, all meals and basic lodge accommodation costs US$266 per person.

A century or so ago, if you'd dropped in unannounced on the Iban people of the Nanga Sumpa longhouse at Ulu Ai, you might have been mistaken for a marauding head-hunter. The longhouse 'drawbridge' would have snapped shut and a hail of poison-tipped blow-darts rained down upon you.

Longhouses are the Borneo equivalent of fortresses. Built on stilts with a single, sealable entry, an entire village of between 20 and 100 families live under one roof in individual family 'apartments', which all front onto a *ruai* (a communal veranda where village life is played out).

The Iban people (who themselves knew a thing or two about shrinking noggins) still live varying degrees of 'traditional' lifestyles in longhouses along Sarawak's river systems. Visiting or staying in a longhouse has become a staple of the Sarawak tourism experience – but with increased popularity, there's often been a loss of 'authenticity'.

A decade ago, Kuching-based Borneo Adventure began operating longhouse tours in conjunction with the members of the Nanga Sumpa longhouse, just outside the Batang Ai National Park. Rather than staying in the longhouse itself, the villagers asked the company to build a lodge alongside so that tourists could sample longhouse life without disrupting the daily routine.

Instead of a flurry of blow-darts, these days you'll be welcomed with a glass of *tuac* (homemade rice wine) and an introduction. The villagers have been encouraged to see tourism as an added extra rather than a staple income, so their main focus is still on fishing and farming – your 'helping hands' will be welcomed!

The few scheduled activities include guided walks through the storybook rainforest of the Batang Ai National Park, where there's a reasonable chance of seeing orang-utans in the wild, as well as other primates and exotic bird life.

It's an unstructured insight into village life on the *villagers'* terms, which is to say you'll be treated as a welcome guest. Someone may even teach you to make a blow pipe.

RESPONSIBLE TRAVEL CREDENTIALS

- **The Batang Ai National Park forest, as with much of Malaysia's jungle, is under threat from population pressure and illegal logging. Tourism provides an alternative income as well as raising awareness – and vigilance – among both tourists and locals.**

- **Nanga Sumpa is recognised as one of the best examples of village-based tourism in Southeast Asia and has won numerous awards. The concept is now expanding to other longhouses in the region.**

- **An education fund established by Borneo Adventure has enabled students to under-take secondary and – for the first time – tertiary education.**

- **Generally in Sarawak, longhouse occupancy is shrinking. In the decade since the Nanga Sumpa project started, the longhouse has grown from 24 to 28 family units, an indication of the economic benefits of tourism – and that the traditional lifestyle may survive.**

- **The community tourism committee ensures economic benefits are evenly distributed among longhouse families, and that fair pay is awarded for tourism-associated work. Borneo Adventure also offers financial assistance to individuals for business ventures. One of the most lucrative new activities is a river shuttle service to transfer visitors to the longhouse.**

FACING PAGE: The Iban of Ulu Ai generally don't put on 'performances' for tourists – you get to join in the everyday activities of the longhouse, without artifice.

EAST TIMOR ~ ATAURO ISLAND: STEERING THE WORLD'S NEWEST NATION TO AN ETHICAL FUTURE

BY KERRY LORIMER

JOHN BANAGAN / LPI

W here tourism development is concerned, the people of East Timor – the world's newest nation – are still finding their feet after 24 years of Indonesian occupation. And already there are plenty of foreign 'investors' ready to step in, with promises of ritzy high-rises and hotel casinos.

But on Atauro Island, just north of East Timor's capital, Dili, the Tua Koin resort near the village of Vila has been set up as a model for a more ethical tourism future.

Australian Gabrielle Sampson, who lives on the island, worked with the villagers to set up the Roman Luan organisation, which built and now operates the resort.

Local materials are used throughout – even the sheets are sewn by the village women. Thatched huts front a pretty beach and lagoon, beyond which lie some of the world's best coral reefs.

It's a simple, welcoming place, where days start with a cup of local organic coffee and fresh fruit. From there it's up to you: snorkelling over coral gardens, playing a game of scrabble, hiking through the island's dramatic landscape of volcanic cliffs or up to the mountains, visiting the local craft villages or renting an outrigger to explore the outer reef.

At day's end, dinner is served in the open dining room, with fresh fish and local produce prepared by the villagers.

Tua Koin is a step towards self-determination for the East Timorese. By staying here, you're helping steer tourism in a direction that will benefit the East Timorese people, rather than supporting yet another wave of foreign invaders.

RESPONSIBLE TRAVEL CREDENTIALS

- **Water is scarce on Atauro. The spacious, shared bathrooms have 'dipper' style traditional baths to save water. Water from the bathrooms is cleansed through a reed bed and used on the gardens.**

- **The resort has a recycling programme for bottles and cans, food scraps are composted and toilets are composting. Power is solar.**

- **The resort has been so successful that the Department of Tourism is promoting it as a model to other villages around East Timor, with groups of Elders coming for site inspections.**

- **Following a Tua Koin–led awareness-raising programme, island leaders have now agreed to establish an association to manage tourism development on Atauro.**

- **Profits from the eco-village are returned to the community and have been used for public works such as piping water to the high school and improving the medical clinic.**

- **There is a craft shop at the resort selling locally produced handicrafts.**

WHEN TO GO

May to November is almost guaranteed not to rain. The wet season, December to April, can be very wet.

GETTING THERE

Air North flies from Darwin (Australia) to Dili, or Merpati flies from Denpasar (Bali) to Dili.

Atauro is 34km north of Dili. You can reach the island by boat – there is a government and a community ferry; the resort can help you organise a small charter boat; or book a dive or fishing charter and get the boat to drop you at the island's dock, from where you can walk along the shore to the resort.

There are eight cabins at Tua Koin, sharing two bathrooms, and they tend to book out at weekends – it's best to phone in advance. They cost US$30 per night per person at weekends and US$25 during the week, including meals.

Further information: www.atauroisland.com

INDIA ~ KUMAON:
A SLICE OF UTTARANCHAL'S VILLAGE LIFE

BY KERRY LORIMER

COURTESY OF BANYAN TOURS

Year-round: each season has its own charms.

GETTING THERE

The walk starts from Almora, which is an eight-hour drive from Delhi. Car transfers from Delhi to Almora return cost US$300 per person.

The home-stays have Western-style loos and bed linen and crockery is supplied by Shakti. You'll be a guest of the family – it's a great insight into rural Indian life.

Day walks are around 10km or five hours in length, and range up to 2200m – but the pace is leisurely and anyone of moderate fitness will cope.

A seven-day package, including three nights in a guesthouse and three nights in village home-stays, including all meals, guide and porter services, costs from US$885 per person in a group of four.

In the days of the British Raj, Uttaranchal's cool setting at the foot of the Himalaya served as sanctuary and respite from the searing summer heat of Delhi and the plains below. Tourism has only lately arrived – in a guise that embraces the simple, quiet pleasures of village life.

The Kumaon Village Walk is a seven-day circuit linking a series of home-stays: villagers in the Kumaon region have formed a partnership with Indian-owned travel company Shakti, to refurbish their traditional homes to accommodate travellers. The accommodation is basic – you'll sleep on traditional charpoys (string beds) and mud floors are covered with hand-woven durries – but it's clean, comfortable, and the owners welcome you in to taste a slice of village life as it is.

In Kumaon, days are punctuated by the toll of the temple bells, the seasons run to the rhythms of the harvest – and the Village Walk cuts a similar pace. It begins in the 500-year-old market town and cultural centre of Almora, where the streets are cobbled, houses are roofed in slate and façades and windows are decorated with ornate wooden carvings.

The walk skirts rice terraces where their brilliant emerald meets the sombre deepness of cedar and pine forests, follows snow-melt streams and climbs through forests to ridgelines with jaw-dropping views of India's highest peaks, stretching to the Tibetan border. The intense green is splashed with the pinks and oranges of saris as the women tend the rice fields and, in season, the crimson blooms of the rhododendron forests.

Paths are shared with village traffic; there are teashops along the way for a refreshing *chai* (spicy tea), and your local guide can explain the workings of the mill or the medicinal uses for trail-side plants. The walk also passes several important temple complexes, including Jageshwar, a pilgrimage site dating from the 8th century.

At the end of each day, you'll be welcomed into a village home, to a home-cooked meal redolent with the spices of traditional cuisine.

The last evening of the trek at Jwalabanj kicks off with sundowners in the rose garden followed by a traditional Kumaon dance performed by the villagers, to the rapture of both trekkers and the local children.

The walk is book-ended with a stay at the more luxurious, but eco-conscious, Kalmatia Sangam or Deodars guesthouses, with some fine cuisine – and perhaps a massage for weary walking muscles.

RESPONSIBLE TRAVEL CREDENTIALS

- There is virtually no environmental impact on the villages or trails. Village houses have been minimally and authentically refurbished, using traditional materials and crafts, and food and supplies are sourced locally. There is no electricity and ablutions are by bucket shower.

- The guides and porters are from the local villages and so act as conduits for conversations between travellers and the local people along the trail, as well as interpreting customs, history and folklore.

- Few tourists reach this remote region. Your visit brings in much-needed income, and contributes to the maintenance of the traditional farmhouses. Monies spent along the trail go directly to local businesses.

FACING PAGE: Every corner of India has its own wedding customs, but they inevitably include several days of feasting, ritual and dancing, involving the extended family and the entire village.

Further information: Australia – www.classicsafaricompany.com.au
UK & US – www.mahoutuk.com

Begging: To Give or Not to Give?

Poverty, raw and in your face, is perhaps the most confronting and overwhelming aspect of travelling in developing countries, and dealing with beggars can be distressing, particularly when these people are clearly in dire need and you have only limited ability to help.

Many of the travel experiences detailed in this book can be an entrée for you to make some difference to these people's plight – the trips and projects here ensure your money feeds back into the community and helps to alleviate the poverty there.

But how do you decide who to give to and who not to?

Just realising that you can't possibly help everyone, and making your own personal 'policy' of who you give to and sticking to it, may help you cope.

You may choose to give a few cents to anyone that asks, but how far can you take that?

It can also be argued that this form of 'charity' actually encourages and perpetuates begging. If you've travelled anywhere in the developing world, you will have been besieged by children begging for 'bonbons' or pens – it can only have been well-meaning, but possibly misguided, tourists who instigated and propagated this practice across the globe. In many places, children skip school or are sent out by their parents to cadge from foreigners – in some areas, children and others are even purposely maimed to improve their earning capacity.

Indiscriminate giving by tourists has helped, in many countries, to establish a begging culture that undermines traditional culture and social structures, and almost inevitably eliminates any chance for equitable interaction between locals and foreigners. As a traveller, you're seen less as a human being and more as a piggy bank.

Alternatively, you could choose not to give to anyone – but to refuse s omeone genuinely suffering can border on inhumane.

The best approach probably lies somewhere in the middle – where that middle is, is up to you. You might decide that someone that performs a small service should be rewarded with a tip, or that mothers with children, entertainers, the disabled, and holy men and women may deserve a contribution.

If in doubt, ask your tour leader (if you have one) or take your cue from other locals – they will know who is genuinely in need, and who is hustling.

If you're not comfortable in giving directly, you might consider making a contribution to a grass-roots community aid programme.

If, like many travellers, you bring stationery or other gifts from home, it's strongly recommended that you give them to a responsible adult in the community – for example the school teacher or village head – to distribute, rather than directly to the kids. This helps to ensure equitable distribution, discourages begging and doesn't undermine the authority of parents and community leaders who tell their kids not to accept tokens from tourists.

It's also worth considering the environmental impact of what you bring – how will the kids dispose of those sweet wrappers or used biros? Will those balloons end up strangling some member of the local fauna?

Perhaps best of all, try to give of yourself, rather than your wealth: share a joke or a meal, start a conversation, pull out photos of your kids or home town or play a game.

INDIA ~ LADAKH: THE HIDDEN VALLEYS OF A BUDDHIST LAND

BY GARRY WEARE

Ascending the summit of the Ganda La (4900m) I see ridge upon ridge of rugged peaks heading south as far as the snow-capped Himalaya. I'm on the third day of a trek across Ladakh, the land of high passes on the border of the Indian Himalaya and Tibet. Below me is the isolated settlement of Shingo, a tiny oasis of deep green barley fields perched at the head of an imposing gorge.

By lunchtime, my local guides and horsemen and I set up camp at Shingo village, leaving me free, so I think, for the rest of the day. Wandering above the whitewashed, mud-brick farmhouses an old lady waves her arms at me. She wears a tattered sack over her shoulders, an olive green balaclava is pulled tightly over long strands of grey hair and partly conceals the deep lines across her forehead.

It dawns on me that I am blocking the path to her small stone-walled field. Stepping back, I watch her collecting bundles of grass and tossing them over the wall for fodder for her donkeys. I, too, wave my arms and offer to help. I clamber up the hillside with all the grace of a pregnant yak, collecting bundles of grass and throwing them over the wall. After 20 minutes the work is complete. Turning to me she smiles and repeats 'Julay, Julay' (the Ladakhi greeting for hello and goodbye), before offering me a handful of dried apricots.

I continue trekking for a further week through villages not yet connected by roads; past ancient Buddhist monasteries perched on the top of sugarloaf mountains; through gorges where the elusive snow leopard stalks its prey; and ascend passes where the 'Wind Horse', imprinted on colourful prayer flags, determines my fortune a thousand metres above the grey, swirling waters of the Indus River.

Trekking in Ladakh is an opportunity to experience an ever-welcoming culture on the borderlands of Tibet where the raw, elemental landscape provides a constant reminder that the peaks of the Himalaya are still in the making.

Further information: www.worldexpeditions.com.au
www.australianhimalayanfoundation.org.au

KERRY LORIMER / LPI

RESPONSIBLE TRAVEL CREDENTIALS

- **Although purists would argue that Himalayan trekking has had a detrimental effect on the environment – witness discarded garbage at camp sites, pollution of mountain streams, deforestation – nowadays most trekkers do their best to lessen their impact, which is minimal in comparison with many other tourist developments.**

- **While the 'one pen, one bonbon' mantra is chanted by small children in remote villages, the majority of trekkers are keen to learn something of Ladakh's culture and rich Buddhist history. Following the foot trails immerses you in life more attuned to the turn of the prayer wheel than our own frantic pace.**

- **Trekkers' contributions have assisted Buddhist monasteries that 40 years ago were falling into disrepair.**

- **The payment of camping fees to landowners contributes to village projects while the employment of local guides and horse attendants ensures monies flow directly into the community.**

WHEN TO GO

The trekking season extends from the time the snow melts on the high passes in late May until the first of the winter snows settle in late October.

GETTING THERE

Leh, the capital of Ladakh, is three days' drive or an hour's flight from Delhi.

Sound acclimatisation in Leh (at 3500m) is imperative before undertaking a trek that can extend from three to 30 days.

For information on trekking independently in Ladakh, see Lonely Planet's *Trekking in the Indian Himalaya*.

World Expeditions has several treks, including the Hidden Valleys of Ladakh, a 21-day trip with eight days trekking and 10 nights in hotels. It departs from Delhi and costs US$2725 per person, twin share, including group camping equipment, transfers and most meals. It also does an annual trek to raise money for the Australian Himalayan Foundation.

FACING PAGE: Local Himalayan herdsmen take a paternal approach to shepherding in order to protect vulnerable youngsters from predators and the cold.

INDIA ~ PENCH TIGER RESERVE:
LEARN MOWGLI'S TRACKING TIPS

BY KERRY LORIMER

Rudyard Kipling's *The Jungle Book* has fired fear and fascination into generations of would-be Mowglis. You could imagine back-scratching on a tree trunk with Baloo the bear, or rumbling with your wolf-cub brothers – but it was the tiger, Sheer Khan, who could inspire sheer terror in everyone.

While still officially lord of the jungle, India's tigers are struggling simply to survive. Poaching, mining, human population pressures and pitiful park management threaten to drive them out of the jungle altogether.

There are plenty of tiger safaris in India's more famous national parks such as Corbett and Ranthambore, but it's only fitting that, if you're going to play Mowgli, you should do it in the very place Kipling set his story: Pench Tiger Reserve – formerly known as the Seoni Forest.

Even better, you can learn the tricks of tracking tigers as a game ranger with one of India's leading ecologists, Dr Mohammed Khalid Sayeed Pasha. The seven-day Wildlife Ranger course is run by Discovery Initiatives. Under the tutelage of Dr Pasha and local naturalists, you learn to track elusive jungle denizens – wolves, four-horned antelopes, jackals, gaur (the Indian equivalent of bison), spotted and sambar deer, wild dogs, leopards, and, of course, Sheer Khan – on day- and night-time forays into the forests.

Mowgli-style, you get to share bathtime with the elephants (and their mahouts) that are used on poacher patrols and to carry tourists in the park.

The emphasis of the course is on understanding the broader ecology of the jungle – the plants as well as the predators and their prey.

A major difference between the Wildlife Ranger programme and other tiger safaris is the community involvement. During the course, you'll meet with the Elders of the villages on the park perimeter, to hear the locals' perspective on having Sheer Khan as a next-door neighbour, as well as spending time with the park rangers to get an insider's take on the difficulties of protecting the forest and its residents. It makes for lively camp-fire debates!

RESPONSIBLE TRAVEL CREDENTIALS

- **Tiger tourism is big business in India. On the one hand, tourism is a major reason the tigers and their parks still exist at all. On the other, there is immense pressure from tourism operators in the more popular reserves to increase visitor limits. If this is allowed without improving management or distribution of tourism revenue to surrounding communities, it will inevitably result in increased persecution of tigers from local people who derive no benefit from tigers or tourism.**

- **At Pench Tiger Reserve, there are fewer tourists, and you travel in small jeeps with better guides than the 24-seater bus convoys such as in Ranthambhore.**

- **The Wildlife Ranger programme facilitates interaction and discussion between the participants and local communities, promoting better understanding of the issues and needs of both parties. All community-based activities are paid for directly to the community.**

- **Despite tiger tourism generating huge tourism dollars in India, the money seldom reaches the tigers – or the local communities that must co-exist with them. Hence park management, rangers and villagers have had little incentive to support conservation measures. A significant proportion of the Wildlife Ranger tour programme monies remain in the local region. In addition, the tour cost includes a US$43 donation to Global Tiger Patrol, a respected UK NGO, and a US$25 contribution to Travel Operators for Tigers (TOFT), a campaign to help make wildlife tourism in India more sustainable.**

WHEN TO GO

The programme runs three times per year from November to March. Discovery Initiatives also has a range of other tiger safaris.

GETTING THERE

The Wildlife Ranger course forms part of the Discovery Initiatives 12-day Wildlife Ranger Safari, which also includes three days in the Kanha Tiger Reserve, which has one of the best chances in India of seeing tigers.

The 12-day tour costs from US$3700 per person, departing Mumbai, twin share in comfortable lodge accommodation with full board. The domestic flight from Mumbai to Nahgpur and the guide services are included. Maximum group size is eight – no experience necessary.

FACING PAGE: It's estimated the number of tigers in the world has dropped 95% in the last one hundred years, and they may be extinct by 2010 if conservation measures continue to be undermined.

Further information: www.discoveryinitiatives.co.uk | www.globaltigerpatrol.co.uk
www.toftiger.org | http://projecttiger.nic.in

INDIA ~ VARANASI: INSIGHTS THROUGH YOGA

BY SARAH WINTLE

It had to be down one of these narrow laneways! My nerves were frayed and I had been awake for less than an hour. As I was about to start cursing, an Indian gentleman swayed me down an alley and my eyes met *the* sign: Yoga Clinic & Meditation Centre. Phew!

Here I was in I-N-D-I-A, aka 'yoga capital of the world', about to trade the comforts of my hip yoga studio in Melbourne for the real thing – private tuition with Yogi Prakash Shankar Vyas (Guruji), one of Varanasi's finest yoga teachers.

In a small room, a fan motioned like a watch in need of repair as I sat diligently before my white-clad teacher. The buzzing sounds of the bazaar drifted away…

Before me was a man who was the very incarnation of yoga.

India, so frenetic and densely populated, surely owes its relative peace, in part, to yoga, which has had a soothing effect on its people for centuries. Every Indian has a concept of yoga and its innate value to well-being.

'Yoga is more than asanas (postures) and today we will begin and end with meditation, the ultimate aim of yoga,' Guruji reflected. 'Deep, gentle breaths now.'

We moved to a series of Chandra Namaskara (moon) salutes. I watched as my 40-something (you can *never* tell the age of a yogi) teacher effortlessly stretched, halved his body, touched his toes and then lowered to the floor with his arms outstretched. In a series of Trikonasana (triangle) poses everything was familiar but became more innately purposeful than I had ever experienced.

PAUL BIGLAND LPI

Guruji told me how he had studied with Satya Charan Lahiri, grandson of the renowned Lahiri Mahasaya. 'We don't go from guru to guru. Finding a yoga guru is very difficult. You need to be accepted by the guru,' he said.

Yoga is the elixir of India. A time-old practice, it remains a guiding force across the rapidly modernising nation. Practising yoga here left me with a thirst for knowledge about the country and its people. India had loomed large in my imagination but now it fills a piece of my heart.

RESPONSIBLE TRAVEL CREDENTIALS

- **Yoga is a great way to interact with locals. It will enrich your understanding of the Indian way of life and slip you into the pace of the people.**

WHEN TO GO

India's cooler period from November to around mid-February is most suited to yoga sojourns. The weather is generally pleasant and most ashrams and yoga schools are open.

GETTING THERE

Whether you're a beginner or experienced practitioner, India is a yoga haven. Lonely Planet's *India* is good starting point to the country's main ashrams and yoga schools where drop-in classes are possible. Ashrams are spiritual communities where attendees are generally required to stay for a week upwards and observe a code of conduct. Ashram fees vary. Where no fees apply, donations are appreciated. Expect to pay around US$2 to US$7 for a yoga class (one to two hours).

Yogi Prakash Shankar Vyas teaches at the International Yoga Clinic & Meditation Centre (☎ 2397139; gurujivyas@satyam.net.in), near Man Mandir Ghat, Varanasi.

Varanasi (Uttar Pradesh) is serviced with regular air, bus and train connections.

JAPAN ~ IRIOMOTE:
TREADING LIGHTLY ON THE
'JAPANESE GALÁPAGOS'

BY SIMON SELLARS

MASON FLORENCE | LPI

Responsible travel may be the world's fastest growing travel trend but you'd be forgiven for thinking it hasn't caught on in Japan. Relentless urbanisation has destroyed much of the country's natural beauty; the government insists on hunting whales, despite international outrage; and almost everything is packaged in plastic, even apples. But don't give up your hopes of having a green and clean time – Iriomote island, in the Okinawa group, is among Japan's last true wilderness areas.

Ninety per cent of Iriomote is undeveloped, covered in dense jungle and mangroves, and a third of the island has been designated a national park. Somewhere In among this subtropical wonderland is the famous Iriomote *yamaneko* (wildcat), an endangered species numbering around 100. The *yamaneko* was discovered fairly recently, just as tourism was making an impact on Iriomote, and conservationists were alarmed that an increasing amount of visitors would further decimate the wildcat population (360,000 visitors came to Iriomote last year, staggering considering the island's population is only 2000).

Residents aren't entirely opposed to tourism but they are concerned with Iriomote's fragile ecosystem, especially considering a four-storey resort hotel has just opened on Todomari Beach (a native habitat for the *yamaneko*), despite years of lobbying against it. That's why the Iriomote Ecotourism Association was formed, with a membership of farmers, sea-kayaking guides, scientists, tour operators, government officials and national park representatives, all focused on helping visitors to care for the land.

One of Iriomote's most popular ecotours involves a kayak trip up the Pinai River, culminating in a jungle trek to the majestic, 55m Pinaisāra-no-taki (Okinawa's highest waterfall). Along the way, guides dispense knowledge about mangrove ecology and the crustaceans, shellfish and other marine life that inhabit the nooks and crannies, as well as advice on the significance of Iriomote's seasons (it's considered an imposition for locals to meet visitors during the rice-planting season, for example). Other tours might offer camping for a night or two (participants are taught to recognise the negative aspects of their impact on the environment, and are encouraged to take all waste with them), coral-reef observations or the learning of local customs including food preparation.

As you stare at Pinaisāra-no-taki, humid with jungle sweat, you might just forget for a moment that you're on Japanese soil. But how long before more hotels appear on the horizon?

RESPONSIBLE TRAVEL CREDENTIALS

- **Now, more than ever before, Iriomote is under threat from developers, with environmentalists warning of pollution and side effects from the Todomari Beach hotel – already, the sea turtles that habitually laid eggs on the beach have not returned since the hotel was opened. Iriomote's ecotours provide a different perspective on mass tourism, proving that it's possible to enjoy the sights without leaving a negative impact.**

- **Iriomote's ecotours also counteract the fearsome effects of the 'nature spirits' of traditional lore, charged with punishing those who tamper with the land.**

- **Ecotours sustain the local economy, providing jobs for residents in ways that don't compromise traditional beliefs or environmental goals.**

WHEN TO GO

Okinawa is in a subtropical climate zone, with balmy weather throughout the year. Summer, naturally, sees the humidity rise.

GETTING THERE

Iriomote is 2000km from Tokyo. There's no airport so travellers need to fly to Ishigaki island from Okinawa or Tokyo, then take a ferry (approximately 40 minutes) to Iriomote.

Mayagusuku Eco Adventures offers a variety of tours covering most of the activities mentioned here. Prices start at ¥7500 per person for a four-hour boat trip up to ¥35,000 per person for a two-night camping tour. Book tours on ☎ 81 980 85 6288; some English is spoken. Iriomote has many ryokan (traditional, old-style Japanese inns) and *minshuku* (Japanese-style B&Bs) options – see Lonely Planet's *Japan* guide for further details.

KYRGYZSTAN ~ SILK ROAD:
GRASS-ROOTS ADVENTURES IN CENTRAL ASIA
BY BRADLEY MAYHEW

ANTHONY PLUMMER | LPI

The fall of the Soviet empire left tiny mountainous Kyrgyzstan way out on a limb and its people desperately short of economic options. Community-Based Tourism (CBT) is a tourism initiative that links travellers directly with a network of local home-stay owners, drivers, herders, horse owners and artisans, who supplement their meagre income by offering grass-roots tourism services.

For adventurous travellers and Silk Road romantics, the programme is a dream. Once you've hooked up with one of the half dozen local village coordinators, the world (or at least Kyrgyzstan) is your oyster. Drive out to explore the 15th-century caravanserai of Tash Rabat, trek through the dramatic alpine valleys of Tian Shan, ride horses up to Bronze Age petroglyphs, visit a traditional Kyrgyz eagle-hunter, or make a multiday horse trek to remote high-altitude lakes dotted with Central Asian herders, stopping overnight in yurts (traditional mushroom-shaped felt homes). The coordinators will arrange all the logistics, at transparent, fixed and reasonable prices.

CBT also organises annual folkloric festivals up in the pastures, which offer travellers a fantastic opportunity to witness such nomadic fun-and-games as *udarysh* (horseback wrestling) and *ulak tartysh* (like rugby on horseback, with the carcass of a dead goat as the ball!), plus the mesmerising sound of a Kyrgyz bard reciting the epic poem *Manas* – a quintessential Central Asian experience that you'll be hard pushed to find anywhere else.

Ultimately, it's the network of yurts up in the *jailoo*s (high summer pastures) that offer a unique opportunity to taste first-hand the semi-nomadic lifestyles of Central Asia. You'll probably share a yurt with a local family; you'll definitely get to share in traditional local foods like *ayran* (yoghurt), *kaimak* (cream) and *kymys* (fermented mare's milk), made fresh on the pasture. The scenery is epic Silk Road – high-altitude valleys, towering peaks and pristine lakes.

The herders and home-stay owners who participate in the programme don't work full time in tourism and arrangements are, by necessity, often impromptu, so it helps to arrive equipped with a sense of humour as well as a sense of adventure. It may take half a day to rustle up some horses or to find an English-speaking guide.

Even if you're not up for an adventure, the network of CBT home-stays offers the best accommodation options in the country and a chance to stay with and get to know a Central Asian family.

There are few places in the world where you can travel so close to the traditional lifestyle of a people, tread so lightly and make such direct economic impact. And at around US$10 a day for food and lodging, or US$25 per day for a horse trek, CBT has to be one of Asia's great travel bargains.

RESPONSIBLE TRAVEL CREDENTIALS

- **A horse trek around the high pastures, eating local foods and staying in yurts leaves almost no environmental impact. And yes, everything is free-range in Kyrgyzstan!**
- **You'll gain a deep connection to the Kyrgyz people and their hospitality by staying in village home-stays or local yurts.**
- **Travellers can buy *shyrdaks* (traditional felt carpets) direct from village cooperatives.**

WHEN TO GO

Summer (June to September) is the best time to hit the high pastures, though the village home-stays operate year-round.

GETTING THERE

From the capital, Bishkek, most CBT coordinators are around five hours away by bus or shared taxi.

CBT has a network across the country, with hubs in Bishkek; Kochkor, in the central plateau; Karakol, on the shores of Issyk-Kul; Naryn, along the road to China; Osh, in the southern Fergana Valley; and Arslanbob, in the southern mountains, among others.

It's a good idea to bring a sleeping bag, water bottle and warm clothes, as well as some snacks.

FACING PAGE: The Tien Shan mountains cover about 85% of Kyrgyzstan, so you're pretty much guaranteed to find a 'valley of one's own'.

MONGOLIA ~ IKH TAMIR:
DISCOVERING THE NOMADS
BY SIMON RICHMOND

JUSTIN JEFFREY/LPI

At 10pm, the day's final milking of the horses done, Narun Zetsig is busy in the kitchen *ger* (the circular tent dwellings of nomadic Mongolians) churning curds from whey to make cheese and cream and distilling *tsaganach*, an alcoholic spirit made from fermented milk. Outside, her husband Bat Ochir and son Bat Irdin round up the sheep and goats into the pen, while I entertain daughter Chimge with my struggles over Mongolian phrases and words. She tries her English out on me and infectious giggles fill the *ger*.

So passes the first night I spend on the Ger to Ger expedition. Apart from travelling each day on horse, on yak cart or by foot in the company of nomads through a very beautiful area of Mongolia that relatively few tourists visit, the expedition allows you to be truly involved with nomadic life – from milking the cattle to sampling a typical diet. This can be rough going: try riding a wooden Mongolian saddle for any length of time and you'll see what I mean! But there are compensations.

On day two Bat Ochir leads my steed across a broad grassy valley towards the second night's camp. Our route passes shady forests hugging the shallow meandering river, a centuries-old burial site and an equally aged stone totem carved in the shape of a man. This pristine landscape, dotted by *gers* and wandering livestock, is a timeless Mongolia eons removed from the modern-day craziness of Ulaanbaatar. And yet I also learn that nomadic culture is not wholly stuck in the past. In the evening nomads might relax in front of the television and DVD player, powered by electricity generated from a solar panel. They also love to have photos taken and are thrilled to be able to see the instant results on my digital camera's screen.

Undoubtedly a herder's life is hard and demanding, with summer being a time of comfort compared to the harsh long winters, but I can see why many nomads persist rather than giving up and moving to the towns. The trip makes me appreciate the comforts of my own life while opening my eyes to what herders such as Bat Ochir get out of theirs.

RESPONSIBLE TRAVEL CREDENTIALS

- **Tour groups are kept small, generally no more than four or five people, and minimum environmental impact principals are followed.**

- **While participants learn about nomadic life, the herders, whose livelihoods have consistently been threatened by natural disasters, are receiving a much needed alternative source of income. An extra incentive is also created for the nomads to preserve their culture, the landscape and historical sites that many visitors come to Mongolia to see in the first place.**

- **Financed by the Swiss Agency for Development and Co-operation, Ger to Ger is a not-for-profit enterprise. Some 65% of the cost of a trip goes back to the herders and community projects.**

WHEN TO GO

From June to September.

GETTING THERE

Tour participants need to get to Ikh Tamir, roughly 500km west of Ulaanbaatar, either by public or self-arranged private transport. It's an uncomfortable trip, along roads that are often little more than rubble strewn tracks snaking across the landscape, taking anything up to and beyond nine hours.

Bring a tent and sleeping bag to camp beside the *gers*, and enough food for a week's worth of lunches and to supplement the very bland nomadic diet – mainly milk products such as cheese, dried curds and sour yoghurt with some homemade noodles and dried mutton thrown in for dinner.

Seven-day trips cost US$150.

FACING PAGE: The Arhangai province of Mongolia is known as the 'horse-breeder's paradise' for its lush and beautiful pastures. You'll live alongside some of the last true nomads – but you might have to share your horse.

MONGOLIA & NEPAL ~ BALDAN BARAIVAN:
REBUILDING TEMPLES
BY SIMON RICHMOND

BILL WASSMAN | LPI

JERRY GALEA LPI

For 240 years the Buddhist temple and monastery Baldan Baraivan stood in a beautiful valley where the steppe meets the Siberian foothills, homeland of Mongolia's most famous son, Chinggis Khan. From its establishment in 1700, Baldan Baraivan (meaning pile of rice) grew into the third-largest monastery in Mongolia, home to 5000 monks. But in 1937 the ruling Communist authorities forced the monks into labour camps or the army and destroyed the buildings and all their contents. Nobody was allowed to set foot on the site for 60 years.

Today, some 15 years after Communist rule ended in Mongolia, the reconstruction of the temple is close to completion thanks to the efforts of the local community and the California-based, non-profit organisation Cultural Restoration Tourism Project (CRTP). The project's founder, Mark Hintzke, heard of the Baldan Baraivan community's efforts to attract international involvement in the rebuilding of their temple in the late 1990s and thought it would be the ideal project to kick off this idea of helping communities around the world preserve culturally important buildings through responsible tourism. CRTP arranges for small groups of tourist-volunteers to pay to take part in restoration projects, which help create jobs for locals as well as allowing the transfer of skills and cultural interaction at a very personal level. Unfortunately, work on Baldan Baraivan has currently ceased due to problems with the provincial government.

CRTP is now focussing its efforts on Nepal. In 2004 CRTP was invited to start its second temple reconstruction of Chairro Gompa, in the north of Nepal, working with the local community and John Sanday Associates (the restoration architects also helping to restore Angkor Wat in Cambodia). The centuries-old Chairro Gompa was once the religious center of the Takhali people of Mustang.

When the Chinese government closed the border to Tibet, the villages along the trade route met with economic hardship and many families left the region. The dwindling population found it difficult to support and maintain the monastery. In the early 1970s the last of the monks left and the fate of Chairro Gompa and its treasures (including wall paintings and sculptures) was left to the elements. CRTP participants are working alongside locals to revive this important relic and restore it as an operating monastery once again.

RESPONSIBLE TRAVEL CREDENTIALS

- **The projects are helping to restore historically important buildings and increasing understanding of Buddhist culture.**

- **CRTP is a non-profit organisation. Over 80% of the revenue raised by its tours goes back into its restoration projects and the communities they benefit.**

WHEN TO GO

The Chairro Gompa project (set to finish in 2011) currently hosts groups in June, September and October.

GETTING THERE

Transfers from Kathmandu to Chairro Gompa are provided by CRTP.

In Chairro volunteers stay with local families in the village. Bring your own sleeping bag.

A 12-day trip to Chairro is US$2495, including transport within Nepal, accommodation and all meals.

FACING PAGE: Many of Mongolia's Buddhist temples are in decay following years of neglect under the Communist regime.

NEPAL ~ ROLWALING VALLEY:
A WALK ON THE WILD SIDE
BY ROD GRIFFITH & KERRY LORIMER

COURTESY OF ROD GRIFFITH

Since the heady days of the hippie trail, trekking in Nepal has been high on the list of the intrepid traveller's to dos. Regrettably, many trekking routes in Nepal have been virtually loved to death: crowding, erosion and deforestation have decimated once-pristine regions. But there are areas that see few trekkers and where the natural beauty can be preserved – if it's managed carefully.

The Rolwaling is a rarely-trekked and little-known valley bordering Tibet, west of the Everest region in Nepal. It has its fair share of huge mountains, but its uniqueness lies in the extraordinary variety of scenery, climate and cultures.

You start off walking in tropical warmth alongside the raging rapids of the Tamba and Bhote Kosi Rivers. Vivid green paddy fields, banana palms and glittering waterfalls give way to rhododendron and oak forests, while the wildlife ranges from domestic water buffalos and goats to Rhesus monkeys, squirrels and butterflies. The local human population changes from Brahmin and Chetri Hindus to Tamang and Sherpa Buddhists as the trek gains altitude and snow-capped mountains make their appearance.

Before you know it, you're above the tree line. The village houses are now built of stone rather than timber, there are Buddhist monasteries adorned with brightly coloured prayer flags and you are at altitudes that most people will never experience. The Tibetan border is a stone's throw away and you are now looking *across* at 7000m Himalayan mountains, not up at them.

From its tropical beginnings, at the high point of the trek you can be walking in snow and gazing down on clouds hundreds of metres below. It's a trek that offers a good challenge, even to the very fit. The mountain views are first class, there's plentiful wildlife and remote wilderness, and along the trail you'll meet traders and pilgrims whose ancestors have been following this route for centuries.

And if you want even more of a challenge you can climb Ramdung or Yalung Peak.

RESPONSIBLE TRAVEL CREDENTIALS

- **Forward-thinking local communities have built environmentally friendly toilets in designated camping areas along the trails. All electricity is generated by solar or hydro. There are no roads, so the only way in is on foot.**

- **Trekking in this area brings employment to local people. Porters are all from this region, and if you plan to cross the Tesi Lapcha it is important to go across with a guide from Na. Fees from designated camp sites are returned directly to the local villages.**

WHEN TO GO

October and November is post-monsoon and everything is emerald green and lush. In April you can trek through forests of crimson rhododendron. December to March is too cold for the higher regions.

GETTING THERE

From Kathmandu you catch the Jiri bus and you get off at Chariokot after seven hours. From there it's a further 10km to Dolakha where the road ends and the trek begins.

Because of its access to Tibet, the Rolwaling Valley requires a special permit. This makes the trek more difficult to organise, however it guarantees that you will be trekking away from crowds. If you wish to organise this trek yourself you will need to purchase a climbing permit (US$300) for Ramdung Peak from Nepal Mountaineering Association in Kathmandu. The permit usually takes two days to organise and must be done in person in Kathmandu, with your passport. Even if you have no intentions of climbing the mountain, this is required for trekking in the area. Trekking without the appropriate permits can incur a fine of US$10,000.

It's easier to organise this trek via a trekking company. Peregrine Adventures has a 20-day trip including a 16-day trek in the Rolwaling Valley. It costs US$1840 from Kathmandu, including meals, guides, permits, safety and camping equipment.

FACING PAGE: Rocky mountain high beneath Gauri Shankar – the 7134m peak forms a spectacular backdrop for trekking in the Rolwaling.

International Porter Protection Group

'In 1997, a young Nepali mountain porter employed by a trekking company became severely ill with mountain sickness. He was paid off and sent down alone. It took just another 30 hours for him to die... IPPG was formed to prevent these recurring tragedies.' – IPPG WEBSITE

Over the years there have been numerous similar incidents. Trekking porters, hired to carry loads in the Himalaya, who've become sick en route, have – quite literally – been left to die. It's still not uncommon to see porters struggling under huge loads wearing thongs (flip-flops) for footwear, or shivering and coughing in inadequate clothing.

The International Porter Protection Group (IPPG) is a non-profit organisation dedicated to ensuring porters are provided with adequate clothing (including boots and warm jackets and trousers), shelter and food, appropriate to the altitude and weather conditions, and that they are not forced to carry unreasonably heavy loads. IPPG also lobbies to ensure that porters receive adequate medical care when sick or injured and that trekking companies provide them with insurance. The organisation's primary focus is on the Himalaya, Andes and Mt Kilimanjaro, the most popular areas where trekking porters are used.

Most of the larger international trekking companies abide by the IPPG guidelines. The worst offenders for porter exploitation tend to be unscrupulous locally owned outfits – and independent trekkers trying to cut corners on costs.

If you're planning a trek, be aware of the issues and ensure your porters are treated with the same respect and care that you'd expect for yourself. If you're travelling with a trekking company, ask them if they abide by IPPG's guidelines on porter safety and what equipment and healthcare they provide. Also ask them about the training they provide their trekking staff and how they monitor porter care.

If you're trekking independently or with a small local outfit, IPPG has set up porter clothing depots at popular trail heads, where contributions of useful clothing can be made and independent trekkers can borrow (with a deposit) clothing for the porters on their trek.

Many Westerners worry whether is it cruel, exploitative or insensitive to hire a porter. The work is not easy, nor is it prestigious, but neither is performing manual labour considered demeaning. It is more dignified for a porter to earn a living than to receive charity and employing trekking porters brings much-needed funds into mountain communities – and without porter assistance, we wimpy Westerners would never make it up the mountain. But it's essential you ensure your porters are receiving the proper wages (don't try to haggle them down below the recognised minimum wage), that they're provided with the right equipment and that they'll be properly looked after in the event of illness or injury.

Travelling with trekking staff makes it far more enjoyable for the trekkers – not only will you be able to appreciate the views without the burden of your beefy backpack, but it's a chance to get to know your porters and guides, and to better understand and appreciate each other's world. For many, many trekkers, this has been a life-changing experience.

For further information see www.ippg.net and Lonely Planet's trekking guides.

SRI LANKA ~ UNAWATUNA:
HELPING OUT, POST-TSUNAMI
BY ETHAN GELBER

GREG ELMS / LPI

The contrast between the pristine pre-tsunami beach I first beheld and that same sandy cove four months later was striking. Gone was the practiced invulnerability of a sheltered vacationer's paradise at the southern bay of Unawatuna. Nothing was as it had been before much of the Resplendent Isle's seashore became a place of remembrance for the 30,000-plus lives lost on 26 December 2004.

However, I was in Unawatuna to join scores of people – locals and foreigners alike – labouring in cross-cultural teams to haul rubble from the shallows, gather debris from the beach. A commitment to home had inspired residents to overcome their losses, repair the damage. A burgeoning sense of responsibility had also moved many foreign travellers to do the right thing: put everything on hold, sometimes for months, and volunteer their energy and resources to change lives for the better, others' lives and their own. Travel had brought people together and crisis had united them. Cultural divides had been bridged by common cause. The guiding spirit of travel – to connect disparate communities – had found form.

As a writer living in Sri Lanka, I also volunteered my pen to a local NGO. However, some of the most heart-warming tales of traveller outreach came from the people for whom Sri Lanka was only a holiday haven, but who had taken the country and its citizens to heart and acted instantly to requite the kindness they had received.

Like Cynthia Palermo, an American film and television producer: 'I knew I had to do something, anything to help. I knew I could offer logistical and organisational support to any group willing to accept my assistance. Now that I've done it once, it will be the way I "relax" between shows and not just in Sri Lanka.'

Today, new tsunami recovery projects continue to be initiated as old ones are completed. New volunteers are always welcome. Responsible travellers remain active in Sri Lanka and, more and more, all around the world.

RESPONSIBLE TRAVEL CREDENTIALS

- Disaster damages the land, leaving it littered, uncultivable, hazardous. Cleanups, structured restoration and culture-sensitive development help to put the land and its people back on the road to recovery.

- Some things cut across all cultures; little rewards more than the joy of a community that has made you feel at home in the village you helped resuscitate. Little tops the sense of accomplishment when a traumatised child smiles in the rediscovered safety of a school or hospital where you volunteer.

- In devastated areas, travellers and volunteers live in small guesthouses, eat at local restaurants and rely on other services suffering from the absence of regular business. It puts money directly into the hands of affected people and lifts their spirits.

WHEN TO GO

Sri Lanka is a year-round destination. Beset by two monsoons, in general (but with frequent exceptions), the southwest sees wet from May to August and the north and east from October to January. Inter-monsoonal downpours strike anywhere in October/ November and May. The hill country is always cooler than the tropical coast.

GETTING THERE

Direct flights depart from Europe and throughout Asia. In-country transport is affordable and easy via train, bus or private/ hired vehicle.

Further information: www.cessrilanka.org | www.hikkaduwa-info.com | www.peraliya.com | www.projectgalle2005.com
www.sarvodaya.org | www.sewalanka.org | www.unconditionalcompassion.com | www.volunteerinternational.com
www.volunteersrilanka.org

TAJIKISTAN ~ PAMIR MOUNTAINS: ON THE ROOF OF THE WORLD

BY BRADLEY MAYHEW

BRADLEY MAYHEW LPI

The Pamir Mountains of eastern Tajikistan have long concealed some of the world's most incredible mountain scenery, privy only to hardy mountaineers and the occasional Silk Road explorer. But there's always been a catch: the decade-long civil war, a pile of red tape and its general inaccessibility have kept the area off the traveller's map.

That's starting to change, thanks to a fledgling income-generation project known as the Murgab Ecotourism Association (META). Travellers can now organise English-speaking guides, regional home-stays and jeep hire through the META office in the regional capital of Murgab, massively simplifying travel in the tricky Gorno-Badakhshan region.

The Murgab programme offers yurt stays in several remote and high-altitude Pamiri valleys, along with four-wheel-drive hire to get you there and horses and local guides to help explore the side valleys. The organisation also suggests trips to petroglyphs and pastures, the ancient gold mines at Sassyk, camel trekking to Rang Kul Lake and even an old Soviet observatory perched on the plateau near the upper Wakhan Valley of Afghanistan.

On our visit, the ever-affable Ubaidullah arranged a Russian jeep to take us out to the remote Pshart Valley, an hour off the Pamir Hwy in an achingly pristine alpine valley. We were introduced to a local herding family and soon settled in for the night, chatting over the warm stove in broken Russian, swapping instant coffee for bowls of freshly made yoghurt. We slept in the guest section of the yurt, along with three generations of our host's family.

The next day we set off for the tough hike over the 4731m Gumbezkol Pass, revealing immense vistas over the surrounding high-altitude desert valleys and corduroy green hillsides. At the end of the day we rendezvoused at another yurt in the far valley and met the jeep for the ride back to Murgab. It was perfect, it was cheap, and we knew that the money we spent was going directly to a community that less than a decade ago was facing war and famine.

In a separate initiative, the development agency Mountain Societies Development Support Programme (MSDSP) has established a network of informal village guesthouses throughout the spectacular alpine valleys of the Western Pamir, around Khorog. The MSDSP office there also publishes lists of local households that are willing to take in guests, once again linking travellers and trekkers directly to local communities that otherwise never get a piece of the tourism pie.

Whether you decide to explore the eastern or western Pamir, it's great to know that your money is directly helping communities rebuild their lives. Revel in the knowledge that you'll be one of the first foreigners there, in one of the remotest corners of Asia.

RESPONSIBLE TRAVEL CREDENTIALS

- **Yurts have a far smaller environmental impact than hotels, especially at altitudes of over 4000m.**

- **By staying in a local yurt you'll get an authentic look at the semi-nomadic lifestyle. You can join in chores like herding and butter-making and if you're lucky you'll get to see a yurt assembled.**

- **A shop selling locally made Pamiri crafts in Murgab helps local women preserve local artistic techniques.**

WHEN TO GO

June to September are really the only times to consider at these high altitudes.

GETTING THERE

There are two access points to the Pamir region: from the capital Dushanbe by plane or shared jeep to Khorog and then a spectacular day's drive by jeep to Murgab, or a long day's drive from Osh in Kyrgyzstan. Both routes take the incredible Pamir Hwy and offer up-close views of 7000m-plus peaks.

Accommodation and meals around Murgab cost around US$10 per person and jeep hire costs US$0.25 to US$0.35 per kilometre.

MSDSP guesthouses cost from US$5 to US$15 per person.

FACING PAGE: Tajikistan remains the poorest of the former Soviet republics and many Tajiks adhere to traditional lifestyles, living in felt yurts that can be dismantled and moved to seasonal pastures.

THAILAND ~ BAN KINGKAEW: VOLUNTEERING TO GIVE & RECEIVE

BY PHILIP ENGELBERTS

MARTIN LLADO | LPI

It had been an emotional week and as I took the stairs down to the ground floor where my bicycle was parked for the final ride back to my guesthouse, I was howling… I couldn't bear to be apart from the precious children, their carers and the strong sense of belonging that I'd gained at the Ban Kingkaew orphanage. Returning to the Sydney rat race seemed more meaningless than ever!

The Thai women that look after the children day-in and day-out thought it was all rather hilarious…a Western man in his thirties blithering and sobbing about saying goodbye to what is essentially a 'happy place'. It made them hoot and roar with laughter!

Such is the strength and the magic of Ban Kingkaew orphanage – home to some 60 children from one month to six years of age. All either abandoned, removed from their homes because of abuse and neglect or because they are the children of parents serving long jail terms.

Spending a week in northern Thailand in the orphanage with friends old and new, I became more patient and more at peace with myself. I know now more than ever what is really important in life and what I will choose to put up with – and what I will not!

The first few days were very much days of observation, and once I had gained the trust of the carers and the kids, it all came naturally to me… Do some boxes need to be carried up the stairs? Does little Chan need a nappy change?

All I provided was an extra pair of hands. I wasn't there to do any policy or strategy work or right the wrongs of the world, but what I did instead was feed, bath, play, cuddle and look after children who – through no fault of their own – found themselves without a primary carer.

The unconditional warmth and love that they showed me is something that I shall never forget and the reason that I will not be able to stay away from Ban Kingkaew. Not for selfish reasons, but mainly because I know that my daily presence there does make a difference to the children living at the orphanage – I have never been so useful.

Despite frequently having been to Thailand and claiming a passion for the culture, on this trip I gained a true window into the Thai way of life. Taking a taxi to the local supermarket to stock up on Dettol, anti-mosquito oil and nappies for your holiday companions is so much more rewarding than gazing at a 'native' dance routine in a five-star hotel lobby!

My return to Sydney was tumultuous…I felt restless and was instantly bored when people started to tell me about their problems getting their car repaired or not being able to buy un-pasteurised cheese! I have made a steadfast decision to return to the orphans of Ban Kingkaew and to make a difference to their lives through fundraising activities.

RESPONSIBLE TRAVEL CREDENTIALS

- **Providing an extra pair of hands – and some much-needed cash – can make a difference to a child's life. And it's a deep-end-in immersion in the Thai way of life where you'll learn as much – or more – than you can teach the kids.**

WHEN TO GO

When the weather is cooler from mid-October to early March.

GETTING THERE

Currently, Ban Kingkaew orphanage is not accepting foreign volunteers. World Endeavours offers other orphanage assistance placements in Thailand. These start at US$990 for a two-week commitment, which includes meals and basic accommodation.

THAILAND ~ GIBBON REHABILITATION CENTRE: BRACHIATING WITH THE LOCALS IN PHUKET

BY EMMA GILMOUR

Just north of Phuket, on the island of the same name, is a small, but amazing tourist attraction that few visitors get to see – the Gibbon Rehabilitation Centre (GRC).

Located in the Khao Phra Taew Royal Wildlife and Forest Reserve (near the park entrance), the centre is run by volunteers and aims to rehabilitate gibbons that have been rescued from the tourist trade. Before arriving at the centre, these gibbons were generally used as enticements to get customers into restaurants or for tourist photos.

The endangered white-handed gibbon is threatened by habitat destruction and illegal poaching. It is rare to see these creatures in the wild, but at the GRC you get to see them behaving naturally – calling, playing and their favourite activity, brachiating (swinging from branches with their disproportionately long arms).

Gibbons are extremely social creatures, but many of those arriving at the centre have only had limited exposure to other gibbons and it can take time for them to be resocialised. An important job for the volunteers is to play matchmaker. This is done through the tried-and-true technique of noticing furtive glances and the not-so-discreet calls that love-struck gibbons make to each other. Once a potential match has been noticed, the gibbons are placed in the same cage and usually become inseparable.

The centre is run entirely on donations and has a small gift shop where you can buy T-shirts, bags and other souvenirs – all the money goes back into the centre. For a more long-term approach you can 'adopt-a-gibbon' for US$36 or you can become a paying volunteer (see website below).

RESPONSIBLE TRAVEL CREDENTIALS

- The twin aims of the GRC are to educate Thai and international visitors and to rehabilitate the gibbons, so that they can be reintroduced into the rainforests, where poaching has rendered them near-extinct.

- The GRC seeks out the support of the local community through school education programmes and by providing free veterinarian treatment. In the future, the aim is to start ecotours where tourists stay with local families and participate in everyday activities such as fishing. This will give tourists an authentic experience and provide locals with a reliable income.

- The GRC depends upon the cooperation of local park rangers to protect the park from poachers. It is located inside the Khao Phra Taew Royal Wildlife and Forest Reserve and the US$5 park entry fee contributes to the employment of the rangers and the protection of the reserve.

WHEN TO GO

The best time to visit Phuket is between November and April. The centre is open daily between 9am and 4pm.

GETTING THERE

Phuket international airport is 30km north of Phuket with daily flights to Bangkok.

The GRC is near the Bang Pae Waterfall in the Khao Phra Taew Royal Wildlife and Forest Reserve. From the airport follow the signs to the Heroines Monument, turn left onto road 4027 and follow the signs to the centre.

FACING PAGE: Gibbons are the best-adapted apes to arboreal life, swinging through the upper canopy – sometimes clearing 6m in a single swing – and rarely descending to the forest floor.

Further information: www.warthai.org/projects/grp.htm

Australia & New Zealand

AUSTRALIA ~ CAPE LEVEQUE:
KICKING BACK AT KOOLJAMAN
BY KERRY LORIMER & BRIDHE MCGRODER

There's snorkelling (A$6 gear hire), swimming and, between July and October, migrating humpback whales put on a display within viewing distance from the beach.

If that sounds like over-exertion, just kick back and relax on the shell-strewn sands of deserted beaches. And when you tire of the astonishing daytime colours, wait for sunset and moonrise, when the entire landscape is suddenly steeped in violet and vermilion.

RESPONSIBLE TRAVEL CREDENTIALS

- **All members of the One Arm Point and Djarindjin communities are shareholders in Kooljaman. Currently, there are professional managers assisting the operation and providing training for local people; however, the vision is for Kooljaman to be self-sufficient and totally owned and operated by the Bardi people.**

- **The construction of Kooljaman follows low-impact environmental guidelines. Ongoing projects include tree planting, recycling and the construction of boardwalks to protect the sand dunes.**

- **All profits are returned to the community, and Kooljaman is nearing self-sufficiency.**

The primal, primary colours of Cape Leveque are hardened in the retina-searing Kimberley sunlight to a simple palette of red Pindan rock and talcum-white sand set against Cerulean sea and sky. Stark. Surreal. Stunning.

And remote. At around 220km and a gruelling three-hour dirt-road drive north of Broome on Australia's northwest coast, the Cape ranks with the most isolated – and jaw-droppingly beautiful – spots on earth. It's not the sort of place you'd wander off in without some solid local knowledge.

Which is what the local Bardi people are bringing to one of Australia's most successful indigenous tourism ventures. Kooljaman at Cape Leveque is a wilderness camp offering a variety of accommodation ranging from camping and staying in traditional palm-frond shelters to sophisticated safari-style tents. Kooljaman is owned jointly by the Aboriginal traditional owners from the local One Arm Point and Djarindjin communities.

From the beginning, the vision for Kooljaman was for a low impact development owned and managed by the Bardi people, which provided employment opportunities for the community in ways that suited the individual members.

Linking in with the accommodation experience, Bardi locals have set up supporting tourism services that take inspiration from the Bardi's heritage as 'saltwater people'. Hook up with a local to go mud-crabbing or fishing the traditional way; listen to stories old and new while out looking for bush tucker. Cook up your catch on the barbecue or dine at Dinkas restaurant.

WHEN TO GO

April to October is ideal; whale-spotting is best from July to October.

GETTING THERE

Kooljaman is around 220km north of Broome, Western Australia. Access is either by air (light plane from Derby or Broome) or by four-wheel drive. The drive takes three hours and you'd be advised to have previous four-wheel-drive experience and to be prepared for breakdowns – there isn't a lot of passing traffic.

Kooljaman has accommodation (and activities) for all budgets. At the top end, safari-style tents are set high on the hill with spectacular views, comfortable beds, kitchenette, balcony with barbecue and en suite bathroom. They cost A$105 per person, per night, twin share. Minimum two-night stay. There are also one-room family units, log cabins and traditional palm-frond shelters set at the water's edge. On the cheap, you can pitch your own tent for A$16 per night per adult, A$8 per child (three to 16 years), plus A$5 per night for power.

There is a small general store selling basic items, open from April to October, but it's advisable to bring some supplies from Broome.

An Indigenous Australian Perspective

AN INTERVIEW WITH KAREN JACOBS

Aboriginal tours try to involve the six senses. For example, on bush tucker walks and talks, we show and tell travellers about our culture and invite them to participate, but we also try to let them feel and understand the spiritual connection to the land. To do this, we prefer to take smaller groups and we respect the environment and communicate our culture. Indigenous tourism is a great example of sustainable tourism.

On an indigenous tour, we don't tell the whole story, we don't show everything: tourists see just the tip of the iceberg. By holding something back, and not exploiting sacred sites and *stories*, we preserve our cultural integrity.

Whenever traditional owners, Elders and tour operators get together, we talk about how to preserve, protect and maintain the authenticity of Aboriginal culture in the tourism industry – how to avoid exploitation and overdevelopment.

Aboriginal people have always been good custodians of the land and have a clear concept of the boundaries that need to be set to preserve environmentally and culturally sensitive areas and sacred sites.

This comes from our inherited connection to the land, rather than something learned. We'll fight tooth and nail to prevent overdevelopment.

We want to share our knowledge and invite people into our country, but there are many obstacles to overcome, from the government, from the industry, from our people and from the tourists.

Many tourists come to Australia expecting to meet a 'real' Aboriginal person. They have this preconception of how that person is going to look and how they're going to act. This is totally unrealistic. There is a huge diversity of Aboriginal people – there are 375 language groups and 600 dialects – and all these people are different, of different skin groups, cultural groups and lifestyles. So you can't generalise – you can't take us as a single group state-wide, much less country-wide. Aboriginal people and the tourism experience will be different from state to state and from one experience to the next.

I'm very passionate about the future of Indigenous tourism. Indigenous tourism has the potential to be Australia's unique tourism offering – nowhere else in the world has what we have.

We have Elders who wonder, 'What could I teach these people?', but when they come back from leading a tour, they're on a high – they're so full of adrenaline we have to have a cool-down session! They're telling their *story*, their sense of place in their country. They are so surprised that people want to hear what they have to say – and that people are prepared to pay to listen. It has such a huge and positive impact on their sense of pride and self-worth.

Tourism is the *only* industry that demands of Aboriginal people that they maintain their traditional ties and cultural practices and share their cultural heritage with the public. It demands that we become business-wise and progress our culture into the future.

And there's something in it for everyone. Tourism can provide business outcomes for smaller families taking tours in very remote areas, which enables them to sustain their lifestyle. In the larger communities, income from tourism is reducing people's reliance on government wage assistance. As it develops, tourism filters out and encourages self-reliance throughout the whole community. Not everyone has the personality to be a tour guide, but everyone that wants to can find their niche – servicing tourist cars and buses as mechanics; running fishing charters or retail outlets; providing accommodation. In the off-peak season, some communities in the Kimberley are providing emergency rescue services for tourists who get stuck up there in the Wet!

Up there, in the Dampier Peninsula, tourism is providing careers – kids come out of school and can step straight into work and pursue their particular interest. With the profits from tourism the community has been able to develop other businesses such as aquaculture, fishing charters, accommodation, arts and crafts – they now have quite a diverse economy and aren't totally reliant on the government for income.

And with Indigenous people, they don't just think about 'me' and 'my' business. They're thinking, 'how can I help my community?' They're not just looking for the immediate rewards – they're considering the wider effects and how to keep going into the future. Before, a lot of people had a laissez-faire attitude to tomorrow, but now they are *living* for tomorrow. It's made a big difference. It changes everything.

But not all Aboriginal communities want to be involved in tourism: some have been forced to – and the people haven't been involved in the decision-making – and these tend to be the ones where tourism is not operating successfully. The people have to want to be a part of tourism and they have to be able to see the long-term, as opposed to just the short-term benefits, which is an educational process. They need to see how tourism can evolve and turn their cultural practices into income-generating businesses. People have to be able to choose the level and the balance of their involvement – otherwise tourism can split the community.

There's a lot of substance abuse and other social problems in many communities – the people have lost their connection to their land and so have lost their identity. It's often the women Elders who take control, and turn to tourism as an opportunity for a solution.

So much goes on behind the scenes just to get an Indigenous tourism venture up and happening, much less operating successfully. I take my hat off to the successful businesses because they've really gone through some hoops to get there.

Karen Jacobs is a Bibbulmun woman of the Ood-da-kalla group of Perth, Western Australia, and is the great, great granddaughter of King Yellagonga. She is the managing director and owner/operator of Kwillana Dreaming Indigenous Tours and Kwillana Mia Gallery. She is a director of Tourism Australia and the vice-chairperson of the Western Australian Indigenous Tourism Operators Committee (WAITOC).

AUSTRALIA ~ INGRAM ISLAND:
RODEO TURTLES FOR RESEARCH
BY KERRY LORIMER

IAN BELL/EARTHWATCH

WHEN TO GO

The volunteer projects run for two weeks, with two projects usually scheduled during July and August.

GETTING THERE

A charter flight departs Cairns for Lizard Island, with an eight-hour boat trip connection to Ingram Island.

You'll need to bring your own tent and sleeping bag. Cooking and other camping equipment is provided. There are no toilets and you get a shower if it rains. You also get to demonstrate your cooking skills – dinner duties are shared.

Share of costs is approximately A$3300, inclusive of all meals, transport, training and accommodation, excluding flights.

Beyond fabled Lizard Island on Australia's northern Great Barrier Reef lies the pristine and isolated Howick group of islands, where serious scientists make like cowboys and the only 'tourists' are their Earthwatch volunteer research assistants.

For the past 12 years, conservation scientist Ian Bell has been working with Queensland Parks and Wildlife to study the critically endangered hawksbill turtle. For part of each year, he relies on 'paying volunteers' to provide the necessary person-power to complete the research. The pay-off for the volunteers? You spend two weeks on a pristine, tourist-free island on the Great Barrier Reef as well as getting up close and personal with some seriously large turtles.

On Ingram Island in the Howicks, Bell and his team – which includes members of the local Aboriginal and Islander communities – use techniques such as the 'rodeo' and 'beach jump' methods to study the leviathans' dietary proclivities. The 'beach jump' is self-evident, while the rodeo involves diving from a moving dinghy, grabbing the turtle at either end of its carapace, and then coaxing the animal to the surface. It sounds rougher on the reptile than it actually is – but it's a necessary evil in order to get a handle on why the turtles are disappearing at the devastating rate of 4% per year.

Bell and co-wrangler Dr Kirsten Dobbs provide all the training you need to be an effective research assistant and you'll also work alongside the indigenous traditional owners. The tricky bits like the rodeoing and laproscopies are left to the experts (Ian Bell has personally inspected the gonads of over 1000 turtles), but you'll nevertheless get plenty of hands-on experience.

The work can be quite tiring, so you get every third day off for snorkeling on the reef and some under-palm-tree recovery. But if Lizard Island is luxury, this is the other end of the scale: This is the most basic bush camping: no showers or loos and whatever you schlep in, you schlep out.

It's rough and ready, but as Ian Bell says, you can derive an immense amount of pleasure knowing you're at a place that very few other people can access and that you're making a tangible contribution towards the conservation of an endangered reptile that has survived on this planet for 600 million years.

RESPONSIBLE TRAVEL CREDENTIALS

- **The Great Barrier Reef has one of the world's largest hawksbill populations. The information gathered so far has led to increased levels of protection where turtles nest and feed, both regionally and internationally.**

- **Over-hunting has been pinpointed as a major contributor to the turtles' decline. An important part of the project is involving Aboriginal traditional hunters in the data collection and helping them develop the skills necessary to sustainably manage their turtle populations.**

- **The project brings traditional owner Elders and younger hunters together on traditional sea country, to discuss and revive traditional hunting methods.**

- **Earthwatch is a not-for-profit organisation. A portion of your share of costs goes directly to funding the project.**

THIS PAGE: Ian Bell measures the carapace of a green sea turtle – they can grow to a metre or more in length.

FACING PAGE: Many species of marine turtles – including this green sea turtle – are declining at unsustainable rates. Volunteers are needed to help figure out why.

Further information: www.earthwatch.org | Other volunteer turtle conservation projects around the world: Australia – www.wwf.org.au | Azores – www.biosphere-expeditions.org Costa Rica – www.anaicr.org | Kenya – www.watamuturtles.com | Sri Lanka – www.i-to-i.com Mexico – www.project-tortuga.org

AUSTRALIA ~ LORD HOWE ISLAND:
BEYOND THE BANANA LOUNGE ~ THE 'OTHER' ISLAND HOLIDAY
BY KERRY LORIMER

WHEN TO GO

Year-round, but best between October and May, when daily temperatures range pleasantly through the 20s. Best birding is from October to November, when the migratory seabirds return to nest.

GETTING THERE

Lord Howe Island is 660km east of Port Macquarie, New South Wales, and less than two hours flying from either Sydney or Brisbane.

Accommodation ranges from self-catering units to luxury lodges (no camping allowed to maintain the tourist limit).

Accommodation must be booked before you leave the mainland – package deals are often the best value.

'**I**t's a one-off, this place, heh,' observes Jack Shick, fifth-generation, laconic Lord Howe Islander, as we top out on his 956th climb of Mt Gower, the 875m basalt monolith that towers with its twin, Mt Lidgbird, over an opalescent lagoon.

It's hard to argue with him. Lord Howe was added to the World Heritage list in the same year as the Galápagos Islands (1982) and, while on a more intimate scale, the wildlife is just as wondrous. You can wade in from the white-sand beach to snorkel with sea turtles and giant sting rays on the world's most southerly coral reef, or float above it in a glass bottom boat while Dean 'Ocker' Hiscox describes the intricacies of a food web that comprises 500 species of fish and 90 species of coral.

If you're of a twitching bent – or even if you're not – the island's bird life is gobsmacking. Like the Galápagos, many of the birds have no fear of man and some – like the Lord Howe Island woodhen – are found nowhere else. Cliff tops give, well, bird's-eye views of swooping red-tailed tropic birds, gannets and boobies.

The island is looped and laced with walking tracks ranging from easy strolls to strenuous climbs (Mt Gower will leave your muscles with fond memories for days afterwards). You can wander through the surreal lime light of a Kentia palm forest or the eerie other-worldliness of a banyan grove, where the canopy of one tree can extend over 11 hectares. The forest abruptly gives way to jaw-dropping vignettes of off-shore islands and sweeping coastal views of black rocks, Prussian-blue ocean, surf, vivid green forests and… incongruously, lush cow pastures.

There are beautiful beaches to lie around on, but if you're looking for banana lounges and umbrella drinks, you're out of luck: the island remains blissfully beyond the radar of the resort pack. The most you can hope for is a slice of powder-white sand without another human in sight…

Just under 400 people live on the island and to move there you more or less have to be 'family' or marry in. The tradition of hospitality runs deep – about five generations in the case of Pinetrees lodge, which has been operating for over 100 years. It's a casual, laid-back place where your hosts meet you at the airstrip in bare feet, no-one locks their doors and everyone has a nickname.

Like the accommodation offerings, tours and activities are locally operated: book a dive to Ball's Pyramid (the world's tallest rock spire, rising sheer from the sea to 550m, and located 26km south of the island); or head outside the limits of the surrounding marine park for some of the world's best fishing (all fish caught are consumed on the island, no exports, no wastage).

In 1935, Lord Howe was described in *National Geographic* as the most beautiful island in the Pacific. Nothing's changed: it's a one-off.

RESPONSIBLE TRAVEL CREDENTIALS

- **Lord Howe islanders and visitors must abide by World Heritage regulations regarding environmental impact. There is a limit of 400 tourist beds, so tourism is never going to get out of control.**

- **The locals take their recycling seriously (what other island offers tours of the local dump?). They'll ask you to separate your garbage and will lend you a daypack so you're not tempted to ask for a plastic bag.**

- **On your bike: pedal power is the way to go.**

- **Most businesses are locally owned and operated – mostly by families who've been on the island for generations.**

THIS PAGE: Banyan and endemic Kentia palm forests cover much of the island.

FACING PAGE: The twin peaks of Mt Lidgbird and Mt Gower tower over Lord Howe's lagoon, which has the world's southernmost coral reef.

Further information: www.lordhoweisland.info

AUSTRALIA ~ MT BORRADAILE:
MYTHICAL CREATURES HIDE IN HONEYCOMBED ESCARPMENTS
BY KERRY LORIMER

KERRY LORIMER

KERRY LORIMER

One day Max Davidson was out exploring in the bush of Mt Borradaile, the 700-sq-km chunk of Arnhem Land in Australia's Northern Territory that he leases from the Ulba Bunidj traditional owners. Fortunately, his footwear – a pair of rubber thongs – wasn't up to the task. As he stooped to curse a flip-flop blow-out, he happened to look up – straight into the jaws of a 6m-long rainbow serpent.

Max was undoubtedly the first white man to see the painting of the mythical Creation creature. He has been the first to see many of the unknown number of rock paintings hidden in the honeycombed escarpments and outcrops of Mt Borradaile, 'forgotten' by the Aboriginal people over generations. Max and current senior traditional owner, Charlie Mulgulda, usually find something new every time they care to look. No-one knows the extent of the work – but most agree it's one of the most important and impressive collections of rock art on the planet.

A 'reformed' buffalo hunter, Max is gruff and grizzled, but he knows his stuff. A stay at Davidson's Safari camp involves heading out in battered, but sturdy, safari vehicles for some 'drive-by shopping'. Max likes to describe the bush as a 'supermarket' and stops regularly to explain the versatility of the native flora and fauna. Green ants, for example, are great bush tucker – they taste like lemon drops, make a refreshing drink and, prepared correctly, act as a decongestant. The morning consists of biting, licking, squashing and digging your way through the wilderness (and experiencing some 'interesting' taste sensations along the way), and traipsing through paperbark forests to reach various sacred art sites.

The Major Art site is aptly, though prosaically, named. Clambering through weathered sandstone catacombs and over rock fig roots the thickness of a thigh, you reach galleries of hundreds of paintings. The works form 50,000-year-old murals, with each generation adding another overlapping layer of history. Rendered mostly in the enduring rust-red of haematite,

the paintings range from simple hand stencils to intricate x-ray style impressions of barramundi, wallabies and stylised humans. More recent works depict Macassan sailing ships and early European explorers.

In the cool of the afternoon the most popular activity is a sunset cruise on the billabong. Four-metre saltwater crocodiles slide from the banks into water so still it mirrors the ridgeline of Mt Borradaile, with its sandstone face reddening in the sunset. The boat glides through lily pads where jacanas (aka Jesus birds) perform their walking-on-water stunt. Over 270 bird species have been recorded and brolgas, Jabiru storks, magpie geese, corellas and clouds of whistling ducks fly in overwhelming profusion across a purple sky.

Eventually, the red lozenge of the sun slides towards its reflected twin; they meet and are sucked into the horizon. For a long, silent moment, there's a sense of connection to the Dreamtime when the rainbow serpent created the world.

RESPONSIBLE TRAVEL CREDENTIALS

- **Max and Philippa Davidson hold the exclusive lease for Mt Borradaile. They work closely with the traditional owners to conserve the art and interpret – and ensure respect for – the traditional culture.**

- **Visitor numbers to Mt Borradaile are strictly limited and by permit only (obtained before arrival).**

- **To visit any of the art sites you must be accompanied by one of Max's trained guides, who are skilled at interpreting both the artwork and the natural wonders.**

- **Davidson's Safari camp is a low impact site that treats its own waste.**

- **As part of the lease arrangement, Davidson's Arnhemland Safaris pays a per-person levy to the Northern Land Council, which distributes the funds among the traditional owners.**

WHEN TO GO

The camp is open year-round. The dry season runs from May to October and is the most popular time to visit, although the wet season (January to April) has its own dramatic beauty.

GETTING THERE

Mt Borradaile is 350km east of Darwin and is accessible by chartered light plane (the preferred option) from either Darwin (60 minutes) or Jabiru (20 minutes). In the dry season, it can also be reached by four-wheel drive – but be sure to advise of your arrival in advance. The Davidsons can arrange your permit and plane flights.

Accommodation is comfortable but basic and consists of twin-share permanent tents with single beds. The ablutions block is separate and communal.

The daily tariff is A$450 per person, including all meals and excursions. There's excellent barramundi fishing and gear is also included. Two-, three- and four-night packages are available but some people stay a week or more. Since groups are so small, excursions are geared to individual interests.

THIS PAGE: Jabiru storks fish the billabong at Mt Borradaile.

FACING PAGE: Max Davidson tells the tale of how he 'discovered' this 6m rainbow serpent.

Further information: www.arnhemland-safaris.com

AUSTRALIA ~ NINGALOO REEF: GOING IN FOR THE KRILL WITH WHALE SHARKS

BY JAMES JEFFREY

The first thing I see is the mouth. Not that I'm immediately aware that it's a mouth; from where I am, hovering just below the surface off the Indian Ocean near Western Australia's Ningaloo Reef, all I can see is a pale hoop emerging from the gloom trailed by ranks of ghostly dots. It's only when it's almost on top of me that it coalesces into the shape of a 4.5m male whale shark. I let out a cry (which promptly vanishes up my snorkel as a stream of bubbles) as it comes level with me and glides by, propelling its improbable bulk with barely perceptible movements of its tail. A comically tiny eye peers out from just behind the mouth, which is opening up to inhale plankton and looks as big as a hangar.

This beast doesn't travel alone. Each whale shark is the living heart of a community of fish – remoras, pilot fish and golden trevally – an armada of tiny escorts that huddle beneath the massive pectoral fins or zoom in and out of that cave of a mouth. It's a lot to take in during the short time available and I can feel my visual cortex starting to do somersaults.

As exciting as it is, it isn't a free for all. There are strict rules and protocols to follow, not least of which is keep out of the whale sharks' way and give them a berth of at least 4m. Flash photography is forbidden and touching is an absolute no-no.

Eventually, the spotted leviathan begins to dive and vanishes back into the dark blue deep. As I crawl back into the boat with my fellow snorkellers and pull my mask off, it's clear everyone's on a serious high. Another batch of whale shark ambassadors has been successfully primed and is now ready to be sent out into the world to spread the word.

On this expedition with Exmouth-based company Ningaloo Blue, we've seen loggerhead turtles, manta rays, jellyfish as big as melons and as elaborate as chandeliers, coral and clownfish, a solitary sea snake sliding clumsily over the waves, pods of dolphins and even a family of humpback whales. As magical as it all is, though, it's the whale shark that's really blown us away. They are the world's biggest fish as well as one of the biggest animals in the sea, yet for all their physical bulk, they're very good at disappearing and keeping much of their life cycles enigmatic – the Greta Garbos of the ocean.

RESPONSIBLE TRAVEL CREDENTIALS

- **Eco-certified company Ningaloo Blue takes its ecological responsibilities seriously, adhering religiously to the conditions of its Whale Shark Interaction licence, which is issued by Western Australia's Department of Conservation and Land Management. Rules include stipulating the minimum distance between divers and sharks, as well as vessels and sharks.**

- **Filming, observation and regular interaction with the whale sharks by the Ningaloo Blue crew adds valuable information to what is so far a fairly scanty stockpile of knowledge.**

- **The tour creates whale shark ambassadors; anyone who's been around one is incalculably more likely to develop some sort of understanding of them and rave about them to anyone who'll listen. Ignorance plays a colossal role in extinction, so it's good to see alternatives on offer.**

- **Ningaloo Blue employs very knowledgeable locals who are evangelical about the marine life of Ningaloo Reef.**

WHEN TO GO

The local whale shark season is April to June, with plenty of sightings in March and July as well. There is a lot of other spectacular marine life year round.

GETTING THERE

There are regular buses to Exmouth from Perth, as well as daily flights to nearby Learmonth. Perth is 1270km to the south, which represents a very solid day of driving.

Ningaloo Blue's full-day whale shark tour costs A$320 per snorkeller, or slightly more for divers. On the off-chance the sharks do a no show, you can go back for free within three years of your original trip.

Accommodation ranges from backpackers and caravans to camping and resort-style digs.

FACING PAGE: Whale sharks grow up to 14m and are found in tropical waters around the world. It's thought they are highly migratory – but no-one knows for sure.

Further information: www.ningalooblue.com.au

AUSTRALIA ~ SYDNEY HARBOUR:
NEW ANGLE ON AN OLD FAVOURITE
BY KERRY LORIMER

COURTESY OF NATURAL WANDERS

S ydney: it's sin city if you want it to be. Brazen and shiny – you can get into as much fun and trouble as you can manage. But if you want to get under Sydney's suntanned skin – or when the hangover's worn off – get out on the harbour and see Sydney from a different (low impact, culturally intriguing) angle.

The harbour is the glittering heart of the city. Most of Sydney's icons arc over it or rim the foreshore – and the best vantage point is from the water.

Hire a sea kayak (or join a guided trip) and take an early morning paddle *under* the Harbour Bridge along the northern shoreline. Paddle past the huge laughing face of Luna Park and the prime minister's pile, Kirribilli House (close enough to offer your personal political statement), and next-door Admiralty House (the governor general's residence). Continue along past Cremorne and Mosman for a gawp at some of Sydney's most expensive real estate. One of the more astounding features of this city of four million people is how much natural bushland – tiny, gold-sand beaches – fringe the harbour. The guided sea kayaking trips include a short bushwalk in the Sydney Harbour National Park and brunch on a deserted sandy beach with some of the best views in town of the bridge and Opera House.

You'd be insane (not to mention illegal) to paddle your kayak *across* the harbour, but you can tack back and forth all day on a yacht. Sydney's yachties are, for the most part, a laid-back bunch and if you turn up at any of the harbour-side yacht clubs on race days with a six-pack in one hand, it shouldn't be hard to find a boat to take you as crew – even if you're just movable ballast. It's a great taste of local 'culture' and a chance to indulge and share in the casual, outdoor lifestyle for which this town is famous. In summer, most sailing clubs host weekday twilight races (different clubs have different days) and in winter Sunday sees the largest fleet in the southern hemisphere battling it out round the buoys.

RESPONSIBLE TRAVEL CREDENTIALS

- **Experiencing the awesome beauty of Sydney Harbour under paddle or wind power is about the most environmentally friendly way to go. Boat owners are obliged to abide by strict environmental laws, such as not pumping on-board toilets in the harbour (although these laws are difficult to enforce) and using environmentally friendly anti-fouling paint.**

- **The yachting scene is very social – it's a great entrée to (and snapshot of) Aussie culture.**

WHEN TO GO

Year-round. Mornings can be cold in July and August for paddlers. Twilight sailing starts with the onset of daylight-saving (last weekend in October) and continues through to March. Winter sailing (May to September) on Sunday is very casual and great fun.

GETTING THERE

Sea kayaking costs A$110 for half a day, including brunch, guide and equipment. Natural Wanders guided trips depart daily from Lavender Bay wharf, just on the north side of the harbour, on the western side of the bridge. There is a limit of six paddlers (plus guide) per trip, so bookings are essential.

There are at least a dozen yacht clubs around the harbour, most of which operate regattas on weekends and on weekday evenings during daylight-saving (summer). Some are stricter than others on security, making it more difficult to actually get to the boats, but generally you can turn up and ask skippers if they are looking for crew (or check yacht-club noticeboards).

AUSTRALIA ~ THE LARAPINTA TRAIL: WENDING WEST THROUGH THE DEEP RED CENTRE

BY KERRY LORIMER

Billed as one of the world's 'classic walks', the Larapinta Trail begins at the Alice Springs Telegraph Station and wends its way 223km west through the deep red centre of Australia, all the way to Mt Sonder. It traces the spine of the West MacDonnell Ranges, one of the oldest mountain ranges on earth. Just knowing these worn, rocky hills were once the height of the Himalaya gives you a sense of the age – and the spirit – of the place.

The trail is niftily divided into twelve sections that vary in length and difficulty: you can choose an easy day walk, a more challenging couple of days, or you could go the whole hog, covering the full distance in a couple of weeks or so.

From the ridgeline you look out over endless plains and red rock mesas – the bare bones of an ancient continent. The trail drops down now and again into narrow canyons and palm-filled gorges that shelter many of the arid zone's rare plants, as well as some of Australia's more fascinating fauna such as euros (wallabies) and perenties (Australia's largest lizard).

Along the way, the trail takes in the established 'attractions' of the West MacDonnell National Park: Simpson's Gap, Standley Chasm, Ellery Creek Big Hole and Ormiston Pound. When you're not tied to the tour bus, you may find you have many of these places to yourself. (Camping under the desert stars in Ormiston Pound is unforgettable!)

You'll have to carry all supplies, including water, unless you're doing a guided trek, in which case a vehicle will drop off supplies along the way.

If you're up for it, you can climb Mt Giles (1283m), one of the highest points in the Centre. Best do it in time for sunrise, when the desert is doused in the unlikely lurid hues of an Albert Namatjira painting. When he first exhibited his work, the now famous Namatjira's colour palette was scoffed at, but spend some time in the desert and you'll see it as Namatjira did.

CHRIS BELL / LPI

It's a trek – and a landscape – on a grand scale and one that lives up to that old cliché: one of the world's classic walks.

RESPONSIBLE TRAVEL CREDENTIALS

- **Trekking the Larapinta gets you away from the tourist crowds and immerses you in the magnitude of this ancient landscape. You begin to feel the 'spirit' of the place and appreciate it from the perspective of the Aboriginal traditional owners.**

- **The two companies offering guided treks observe minimum impact practices.**

- **You need to be totally self-sufficient – what you carry in, you'll need to carry out.**

- **Camp fires are permitted, with care, but park rangers strongly recommend you take a gas cooker.**

- **There are composting toilets at official camp sites.**

WHEN TO GO

It's best between April and October in the cooler months. Days will be warm, nights will be cold.

GETTING THERE

For day walks or to do the walk independently, stock up in Alice Springs and head out (you'll need to take everything, including water). You can access the start of most sections by car. Or book with one of the two licensed operators who have guided trips.

World Expeditions has eight-day and 14-day (the whole hog) trips, with vehicle support (camps are set up and water/food brought in). The 14-day trip costs A$2990 per person, including all meals and camping equipment (you'll be sleeping in swags).

Trek Larapinta has both group and tailored trips led by local biologist Dr Charlie Carter. They range from two to 20 days – the annual 20-day End to End walk costs A$2970, including all gear (swags as well).

You need to be in good shape for the longer treks – these involve up to 10 hours per day on rough terrain.

AUSTRALIA ~ THE TARKINE: WALKING ONE OF THE WORLD'S LAST WILD PLACES

BY KERRY LORIMER

COURTESY OF TARKINE TRAILS

I stood atop a wind-lashed sand dune on the sea edge of the Tarkine, the seashells of an ancient Aboriginal midden spread at my feet. Before me, dark roiling waves beat against billowing clouds. Behind me the unbroken wildness of the rainforest and heathland stretched for almost half a million hectares and across 65 million years, all the way back to Gondwana. I felt like I stood on the fault line of the wildest place on earth.

Trekking the Tarkine is a challenge. If the thylacine (the reportedly extinct Tasmanian 'tiger') still lives, it is surely here in the impenetrable tracts of 'horizontal' scrub and the shadowy depths of the sassafras and myrtle forest where, for the most part, no human has ever ventured.

The Tarkine, in Tasmania's northwest, is Australia's largest tract of temperate rainforest – and the second largest in the world. Essentially undisturbed for millennia, the forest is astonishingly complex. Relics of Gondwana, leatherwood trees and Antarctic beeches – towering up to 40m – form the forest canopy. The forest floor is strewn with massive, moss-covered logs and, where the canopy is broken, shafts of sunlight illuminate delicate tree ferns. There are also patches of heathland and buttongrass plains; wind-strafed beaches; and some of the planet's last wild rivers and streams, inhabited by platypus and giant crayfish.

Incredibly, the Tarkine is still not fully protected from logging and an open-cut mine operates at Savage River in the heart of the forest. Campaigning by grass-roots conservationists, the Tarkine National Coalition, the Wilderness Society and WWF has helped convince the Tasmanian government not to log the sensitive heart of the rainforest. But the threat – both from logging and mining – is not over yet.

The loggers' argument is simplistic: felling the Tarkine equals jobs. The anti-loggers argue that tourism – if carefully managed – can offer a richer and more sustainable economic future.

The first steps towards establishing walking trails along the lines of the classic walks of Tasmania's southwest are being taken. For now, the Tarkine is – literally – a walk on the wild side: so remember to keep an eye out for thylacines.

RESPONSIBLE TRAVEL CREDENTIALS

- **The Tarkine comprises around 450,000 hectares of which only 18,000 hectares is 'permanently' protected as national park.**

- **By trekking the Tarkine, you're supporting the campaign to prove to the Tasmanian government that tourism is a viable alternative to logging and mining. Until tourism can generate proven income for the region, logging will remain a threat.**

- **The system of trails is being developed in consultation with the Tarkine National Coalition and others, using existing trails and with a sustainable development vision that will see tourists keeping to the edges, while the heart of the forest remains untouched.**

- **The Aboriginal middens and archaeological sites along the coast are of global significance. Currently, they are under threat from cattle grazing and illegal four-wheel drivers. You can add your voice to the campaign to have these ancient historical sites permanently protected.**

WHEN TO GO

Trips operate between November and April.

GETTING THERE

The Tarkine National Coalition publishes a self-drive brochure for two-wheel drivers that directs you to walking trailheads. Walks range from a couple of hours or less to full-day and multiday hikes.

Local company Tarkine Trails is run by long-time conservationists and is currently the only operator offering extended walks in the Tarkine. Six-day walks start at A$1045 per person and depart Launceston/Burnie more or less weekly. They also operate a six-day car-based tour.

All tents, meals and camping equipment are provided, but you have to carry it. Expect loads of between 14kg and 19kg – so you need to be reasonably fit.

FACING PAGE: The Tarkine is one of the world's most ancient and important forests – most of it is near-impenetrable. Conservation organisations have had recent wins in securing conservation status, but the trees are not yet out of danger.

Further information: www.tasmaniawalks.com | www.tarkine.org | www.wwf.org.au

AUSTRALIA ~ ULURU: GETTING THE ABORIGINAL PERSPECTIVE

BY KERRY LORIMER

For decades, tourists have been clambering up – and occasionally falling off – Australia's most recognisable natural icon, Uluru (Ayers Rock). Chains were bolted into the rock to aid their efforts and countless 'pebbles' were souvenired. Despite the undeniable spiritual impact on anyone that sees Uluru, few respected – or even considered – the sacred significance of Uluru to the local Anangu Aboriginal people, or their expressed desire that nobody climb the rock.

Anangu Tours, an Aboriginal-owned company operating walking tours around (and not up) the rock, is seeking to redress the balance. Aboriginal traditional owners guide all the tours, speaking in their own language, assisted by qualified interpreters. They relate the myths and lore of the oldest living culture on earth – passed down through generations – that sought to make sense of the landscape they lived in.

On a half-day tour, you'll also learn how to make fire without matches, throw a spear and hear how animal totems such as the hare wallaby and woma python are woven into the Anangu cultural heritage.

The Uluru Kata Tjuta National Park is included on the World Heritage list for both its natural and cultural values, and was only the second national park in the world to be recognised as a cultural landscape.

After hearing first hand – expressed in their own words – the significance of Uluru to the Anangu, you might just reconsider a summit bid.

COURTESY OF ANANGU TOURS

RESPONSIBLE TRAVEL CREDENTIALS

- The walking tours do not go up Uluru as a mark of cultural respect (and for safety reasons), but also to protect the rock's friable surface.

- All tours are led by Anangu people, trained in the correct interpretation of Tjukerpa (Creation law).

- The Anangu community, in conjunction with the Australian Nature Conservation Conservancy, has established a free cultural centre near the park entrance. It's strongly recommended you visit the cultural centre before you visit Uluru, even if you're not taking an Anangu tour. There are excellent interactive displays on Aboriginal culture, nature and history.

- Profits from the company are returned to the Aboriginal communities in the region and are used for development projects including education and health.

WHEN TO GO

March to October is the most pleasant time to visit Uluru – days are warm, but nights are cold. November to February is extremely hot.

GETTING THERE

There are regular scheduled flights to Uluru from all Australian capital cities. It's also possible to drive – accessible by two-wheel drive.

Anangu Tours operates a range of tours daily. Most popular is a half-day walk, timed to experience sunrise over Uluru followed by a walking tour. It costs A$119 for adults and A$79 for children, including breakfast. Pick-up is from your accommodation and the tour lasts approximately five hours.

THIS PAGE: Anangu women will teach you to use their 'tools of trade' for gathering foods and medicines.

FACING PAGE: Every cave and every outcrop of Uluru has significance for the Anangu people. Seeing it through their eyes gives a spiritual understanding.

Further information: www.anangutours.com.au

NEW ZEALAND ~ KAIKOURA:
FEEL THE MAORI SPIRIT OF PAIKEA, THE WHALE RIDER

BY RICHARD FIELD

DAVID WALL | LPI

FERGUS BLAKISTON LPI

'**G**et your cameras ready, he's about to dive!' The captain was referring to the 40-tonne sperm whale that had been lazing not far from our boat for the last 20 minutes. With cameras overheating, the obliging whale lifted his tail, curled it over in a most photogenic way, and promptly disappeared. It propelled itself down with such force that the water was still being displaced minutes after we had lost sight of the animal. The crew, knowing that the whales can stay under for over two hours, ushered us back to our seats, and we took off to find another of the whales that live in the waters off Kaikoura year-round.

Whale Watch Kaikoura is remarkable for many reasons. Firstly, the wildlife experience is phenomenal. Visitors are almost guaranteed to have incredible views of sperm whales, with dusky dolphins also sighted on almost every trip. Some visitors will also be lucky enough to see humpback whales, orcas and even blue whales as they move through the area. Secondly, the guides on board the boats pass on great educational information about the whales, and visitors are even given a glimpse of the Hikurangi deep-water trench – one of the key reasons for Kaikoura's prolific marine life – through a hi-tech, digitally animated presentation. Thirdly, Whale Watch Kaikoura is Maori-owned and operated, and from humble beginnings, the company has grown to be the backbone of what is now a thriving tourist town.

In the late 1980s Kaikoura was just another of New Zealand's sleepy seaside fishing villages in serious economic decline. Unemployment was high, particularly amongst the Ngai Tahu, the local indigenous population. Drugs and alcohol were major problems and there was great tension between the Maori and other members of the community.

Sensing the desperation of their people, some of the tribal Elders borrowed money and even mortgaged their houses, and began taking tours in rubber dinghies to see the great whales that play such an important part in their cultural heritage. Despite wear and tear on the boats and a few tough early years, Whale Watch has grown dramatically, along with the town of Kaikoura.

In 1987 Kaikoura had roughly 3400 tourists a year. Now that number stands closer to 800,000, with close to 100,000 enjoying an up close and personal experience with Whale Watch. More importantly for the Ngai Tahu, they are now highly regarded members of their community, they have jobs and their children have opportunities. Like Paikea, their ancestor and inspiration, the Ngai Tahu are riding high on the back of the whale.

RESPONSIBLE TRAVEL CREDENTIALS

- **The Whale Watch boats observe strict approach guidelines and the guides on board give important conservation information regarding the whales. The boats use inboard diesel engines, which minimise underwater noise, and all toilets on board are self-contained, thus reducing pollution.**

- **The company is Maori-owned and operated, and a significant proportion of the employees are Ngai Tahu. Visitors are also encouraged to experience more of the Maori culture by visiting the Takahanga marae (meeting house) of the Ngai Tahu, located in town.**

- **Whale Watch Kaikoura funds education and training programmes at the Takahanga marae, including programmes aimed at reviving their culture and traditions, which date back centuries. Staff from Whale Watch visit schools in Kaikoura and neighbouring areas to educate kids about whales and their conservation. Free whale-watching excursions are run for these schools in the winter months.**

WHEN TO GO

Whale watching is good all year-round, although the warm temperatures from November through to March make it the most popular time of year.

GETTING THERE

Kaikoura is an easy 2½-hour drive north of Christchurch, on New Zealand's South Island. It can also be accessed by rail or air from Christchurch.

Kaikoura has a large variety of accommodation depending on budget, although it is wise to book in advance, particularly during the busy summer months (December through to March).

The 2½-hour cruise costs NZ$125 for adults and NZ$60 for children under 15. The tour isn't suitable for children under three.

Whale Watch Kaikoura offers an 80% refund if you don't see a whale. Bookings are essential.

FACING PAGE: Humpback whales can be identified by the individual markings on their tail flukes – right before they dive to depths of 200m for up to 30 minutes.

NEW ZEALAND ~ WAIPOUA: A MEETING WITH THE FATHERS OF THE FOREST

BY KERRY LORIMER

Tane Mahuta – the Lord of the Forest – has been holding Earth and Sky apart for over 2000 years. New Zealand's tallest kauri tree has managed to put 51.5m between Rangi (Sky) and Papatuanuku (Earth), which, in the beginning, according to Maori legend, were joined in a coital embrace.

Maori guide Koro Carman tells the story of how Mother Earth and Father Sky were parted, allowing light and life to populate the earth, as he plays a solitary spotlight along the length of Tane Mahuta's grey ghost trunk.

As you stand before his lordship, lapped by the darkness of the forest and the noises of the night, his limbs do indeed seem to scrabble at the stars.

Koro Carman and fellow Maori local Joe Wynyard started Footprints Waipoua to 'add value' to the usual tourist experience of visiting the world's oldest and tallest kauri trees in the Waipoua Forest in New Zealand's Northland. They take guided walks interwoven with ecological interpretations and Maori songs and legends. And they take them at night, when the forest's shyest inhabitants get about their nightly business and the trees' majesty is at its most mesmerising.

Tane Mahuta's mighty 13m girth is testament to the strength required to rend the Sky-Earth lovers asunder. It takes eight people to give the Lord of the Forest a circumferential hug. But on the four-hour Footprints walk, you'll also meet the Father of the Forest, Te Matua Ngahere. While shorter at around 35m, Te Matua Ngahere is even stouter, measuring up at 20m around his middle.

Koro and Joe aim to introduce you to other denizens of the darkness, including kiwis, owls and a multitude of crawling critters. There's no guarantee you'll meet the national emblem, but you will see Gondwanan grandfathers who were already ancient when Kupe, the Polynesian forefather of the Maori, landed in the Land of the Long White Cloud.

RESPONSIBLE TRAVEL CREDENTIALS

- **Waipoua is the world's largest kauri forest, protecting three quarters of New Zealand's remaining kauri trees, which are remnants of ancient subtropical rainforests. Footprints Waipoua is the only company to have a Department of Conservation (DOC) permit to operate both day- and night-time guided walks in the forest.**

- **Footprints is owned and operated by Maoris and aims to educate local and international visitors – including kids from five years old – about forest ecology, as well as the lore and legends of the Maori and the physical, cultural and spiritual importance of the forest.**

WHEN TO GO

Waipoua is a year-round destination.

GETTING THERE

Waipoua is one hour from the Bay of Islands and around four hours from Auckland, on the west coast of New Zealand's North Island.

Forest paths make the walking easy – suitable for just about anyone. Minimum recommended age is five years.

Footprints Waipoua operates in cooperation with the Copthorne Hotel and Resort in Hokianga. Bookings can be made direct with Footprints or via the hotel.

The Twilight Encounter runs for four hours (and 6km) and costs NZ$65 for adults and NZ$48 for kids (five to 12) and departs at twilight. The 1½-hour shortened version, Tane at Night, costs NZ$45 for adults and NZ$33 for children.

Europe

ENGLAND ~ COAST-TO-COAST: ON TWO WHEELS

BY TOM HALL

WHEN TO GO

While winter isn't out of bounds, you'll get the best weather and lowest crowds during late spring and summer, provided August is avoided. Ultimately though, this part of the world is wonderfully green for a reason – come prepared for rain and getting cold on higher passes.

GETTING THERE

Coach (www.nationalexpress.co.uk) or train (www.nationalrail.co.uk) are the best ways to get to the start of the route, and then home again. With notice, most passenger services will carry bikes for free – no matter how grubby they are.

The National Cycle Network has re-invigorated England's lost areas – from disused railway lines to forgotten back-roads and canal towpaths. Set up by Sustrans (as in Sustainable Transport), it is part of ongoing efforts to open up traffic-free routes for cyclists and walkers all over the UK. And you owe them an organically-brewed pint of foaming ale or two, because the very best of the English countryside – 25,800km of it – is now easier than ever to discover, without a car in sight.

Despite the huge choice of routes, few journeys in England offer the unique sense of achievement as the C2C (Coast-to-Coast) cycle ride. The best known of the national routes, it's a 225km challenge through England's most breathtaking scenery and beautiful, off-the-beaten-track spots. The ride has attracted praise from far and wide, and has been showered with best-in-class prizes from the Smithsonian, Gulbenkian and Tourism for Tomorrow awards.

Beginning in Workington or Whitehaven, hugging the coast on the Irish Sea, the C2C rises into the northern Lake District before winding through the north of England and finishing on the North Sea in either the bright lights of Newcastle or surrounded by Sunderland's gritty shipbuilding heritage. Don't forget to dip your front wheel in the brine at the finish, as you wet your back wheel at the start – it's a tradition all riders observe.

Planning a C2C ride is easy. There's lots of accommodation en route, from B&Bs to hostels to camp sites, and while the route passes through high and wild country there are also easy lunch and dinner stops should you wish to travel light. An ordinary hybrid bicycle can handle anything the route will throw at you. While the very fit will do the journey in two days, the ascents and wonderful countryside merit taking three or four days over the journey.

IAN CONNELLAN / LPI

Don't fancy the crowds? Try the equally beautiful Pennine Cycleway, and the northern section in particular for less crowds. Exhilarating, energetic and uniquely English, the C2C is a must for the adventurous wanderer with two wheels.

RESPONSIBLE TRAVEL CREDENTIALS

- On a bike you're being kind to yourself and the scenery around you.

- On two wheels there's time to talk. Locals, cyclists or otherwise are delighted to chew the fat over the weather – a topic that will quickly obsess you as much as them – and points of interest along the way. The route is designed to show off the history as much as the scenery of the area in a sensitive way. C2C riders come away with a sense of how the north of England has evolved, which you can't learn in a museum.

- The C2C passes through former fishing ports, mining villages and farming communities that bear the scars of tough times. The steady stream of hungry, thirsty cyclists brings much needed funds to local businesses.

Further information: www.sustrans.org.uk | www.c2c-guide.co.uk

Taking to the Road Responsibly: On Two Wheels

BY ETHAN GELBER

For 20 years my desire to see the world from the saddle of a bicycle has been unquenchable. Touring on two wheels is, for me, the only way to travel. Deep in the wilderness and on the roads, over long and short hauls, in the familiar and the foreign, it just can't be beat, especially as a responsible form of transportation. It works wonders for your emotional and physical wellbeing. It saves on transport costs. And, of course, it does little to damage the environment or sap its resources, adds no noise to natural calm, no pollutants to pure beauty and no danger in protected places.

Bicycle tourism also fells many of the obstacles that sometimes keep visitors and locals apart. Better yet, it actually creates commonality. As a cyclist you can choose paths that wander far from motorways, putting you in touch with people in places that outsiders don't see. When you're hungry, you can pause in small markets patronised only by locals. When it rains on field workers, you get wet with them or share their shelters. Plus, you develop a healthy respect for the land, one that teaches both humility and forbearance.

Short pedal trips are a more and more common traveller's treat, whether shopping near home or renting a steel steed for a zip to a nearby attraction. Long trips and involved adventures are the makings of journeys of a lifetime. Both are responsible forms of travel gauged to a human pace, more resonant with nature, the elements and the people who live by their rhythms.

As the world gets smaller and distant horizons creep closer, a new breed of robust cyclist has flourished: one ready to push over distances that even some motorists would balk at – hundreds and sometimes thousands of kilometres, tackled over lengthy stretches of time.

My list of top 10 epic bike tours, in no particular order, is truly epic. Don't think, 'I could never do that'. You'd be surprised how many journeyers do – those who let fancy and curiosity get the better of them.

TOP 10 EPIC BIKE RIDES

- **Silk Roads** – any of the famous ancient trade routes from the Middle East, across Asia to China
- **Iberian Pilgrimage Routes** – the Camino de Santiago between French starting points and the Spanish city of Santiago de Compostela
- **Crusade Routes** – any of the well-trampled roads between Western Europe and the Middle East, perhaps along the path of the Orient Express or the Via Egnatia
- **In Napoleon's Wake** – a transcontinental pedal from Paris to Moscow
- **Around the Mediterranean** – from Morocco to Spain, the long way, keeping near the coast
- **Extended Rift Valley** – a trip along this great cleft in the world, from the Jordan River along the Dead Sea into East Africa
- **Australian Coast** – a 25,750km odyssey keeping within sight of the wet part of this dry continent
- **Coast-to-Coast USA** – the 6840km TransAmerican Trail, the 6945km Northern Tier, or the 5120km Southern Tier
- **Great Divide Route** – a 3975km off-road adventure that runs along or near America's craggy cleft dividing the watersheds east and west
- **Pacific Coast Hwy** – all or a big part of the whole highway from Alaska to Tierra del Fuego

FINLAND ~ OULANKA NATIONAL PARK:
HIKING AMONG THE CLOUDBERRIES
BY RACHEL ALT

DAVID TIPLING LPI

WHEN TO GO

Mid-summer is from May to July, and provides hikers with almost 24-hour sunlight.

GETTING THERE

Lapland is the northernmost area in the EU and includes northern Norway, Sweden, Finland and Russia. It is largely within the Arctic Circle.

Oulanka National Park is located 50km north of the town of Kuusamo. Public buses run to and from the park daily. Entry to the park is free.

Flights from Helsinki to Kuusamo with Finnair depart daily and take 1½ hours.

Bring your own sleeping bag and food, as there is no means of purchasing provisions once inside the park.

Mosquitoes can pose a problem, so pack repellent for during the day and a mosquito net for a comfortable night's sleep.

Nestled in the Arctic heartland, where reindeer roam, cloudberries flourish and local Lappish inhabitants have freely trekked the tundra for centuries, is some of the best free accommodation in which a weary hiker could spend a night.

Originally built for reindeer herders across the northern Finnish landscape, wilderness huts have provided refuge for hikers and herders since the early 20th century. The huts remain unlocked, most require no reservations or advance bookings, and are maintained by the Finnish Metsahallitus (Forest and Park Service). Hikers are welcome to use them, provided they abide by a few simple rules: leave the hut as you found it, with firewood chopped and stacked by the stove; keep it clean; and leave a message in the guest book.

The huts range in sophistication from sturdy log cabins to rustic lean-tos. Facilities can include bunks for sleeping, cookware, a stove, table, benches and dry toilet. Occasionally a gas cooker will be provided, and often an axe and saw to chop firewood are available. The locals preserve a 'wilderness rule', which dictates that the last to arrive gets the best bunk.

However, bunk-right conflicts are rare considering that in the wildest parts of northern Finland hikers can wander for hours – or even days – without seeing another soul. The terrain is so remote and untouched that some locals advise hikers to wear bells at their waist to warn resident bears of their approach.

You can pick wild berries and mushrooms along hiking trails – provided the local reindeer don't beat you to them. As warmer weather melts the winter snow, fish thrive in the churn of world-class rapids.

Finland is home to 35 national parks and Lapland is home to over 48,000 sq km of the best-preserved wilderness in Scandinavia. Unrestricted access is granted by virtue of Everyman's Right – a centuries-old good-will code that means anyone can roam freely over any land, without the landowner's permission.

The Bear Ring in Oulanka National Park offers some of the most spectacular forest hikes (fell-walking) in Finnish Lapland. Paths carpeted with pine needles follow streams through ancient forests and over gentle hills. For most of the time you're enveloped by the serenity of the forest, with views glimpsed through the trees or from suspension bridges crossing swift-flowing rapids.

Trails range from the 1km children's Troll Hike, to day trips of around 12km and up to the Karhunkierros Hiking Trail, which stretches across 80km and is most comfortably walked in between four and six days. Trails in the region are serviced with nine open wilderness huts.

RESPONSIBLE TRAVEL CREDENTIALS

- **In 2002 Oulanka National Park was awarded a PAN Parks (www.panparks.org) certificate, which recognises the park's success in balancing nature conservation and the increasing pressures of nature tourism.**

- **Hiking the Arctic tundra, staying in wilderness cabins and observing the wilderness rules and Everyman's Right preserves traditions hundreds of years old.**

GREENLAND ~ TASIILAQ: ARCTIC EXPLORATION ON THE GREENLAND ICECAP

BY ETAIN O'CARROLL

If you've ever harboured secret fantasies about becoming an Arctic explorer, being buffeted by fierce winds, caught in blizzards, and stuck in a makeshift snow hut for days on end, but in reality can't get away from your day job and don't really like the cold, this is the trip for you.

Covering almost 85% of the largest island in the world and in places almost 3km thick, the Greenland icecap is one of the most spectacular places on earth. In a 'white out' the sky becomes indiscernible from the surface, visibility is reduced to a few metres and the chilling silence can be haunting. On a clear day it is simply stunning.

One of the easiest places to access the icecap is the small, isolated and traditional community of Tasiilaq in East Greenland, where Robert Peroni runs the Tuning Incoming Agency, a socially and ecologically conscious tourism project. The agency works hard to provide jobs and opportunities for local people and yet attempts to preserve the identity of East Greenland and its inhabitants despite the influx of day-trippers in the summer months.

Tuning doesn't run set trips, but tailors each low-impact tour to guests' needs and experience levels. This can mean anything from advising experienced mountaineers on routes, safety, equipment and supplies, to providing a fully guided mountaineering expedition on little known peaks, or a multiday trip across the icecap.

With equipment, routes, boat transfer and pick-up all organised, all you need to do is make your way up and onto the icecap and enjoy the incredible scenery and the ultimate sense of space and silence.

GRANT DIXON | LPI

Tuning also organises kayaking trips through iceberg-littered bays to local glaciers, shorter day hikes and boat trips. Wherever possible local hunters are employed as guides, and for overnight trips accommodation can be arranged with local families in small outlying villages.

RESPONSIBLE TRAVEL CREDENTIALS

- Tuning employs local hunters but limits the number of hours they can work so that their official status as hunters is not lost.

- The agency provides training and support to vulnerable members of the community.

- Arriving by boat, travelling on foot, or paddling a kayak makes negligible environmental impact compared with the helicopter tours run by local hotels.

WHEN TO GO

For the best combination of weather, reasonable temperatures and long days, late spring is a good time to travel. Later in the summer much of the snow has melted but Kong Oskar Havn will be full of glittering icebergs. Autumn sees a dramatic change in colour, and for extreme weather conditions, dog sledding, snow-shoeing and spectacular displays of the aurora borealis, late winter and early spring are the time to go.

GETTING THERE

You can arrange all travel to Tasiilaq yourself or Tuning Incoming can make international bookings for you.

International flights are available to Kulusuk (East Greenland) from Keflavik (Iceland) or from Copenhagen (Denmark). From Kulusuk it's a two-hour boat ride or a 10-minute helicopter trip to Tasiilaq. Tuning attempts to get all guests to Tasiilaq by boat, giving visitors an authentic first impression of Greenland, where boats are the most common form of transport.

To take an expedition to the icecap you need to be reasonably fit and have some mountaineering experience. Other trekking expeditions in the area require less experience.

Budget on spending about US$130 per day for guided hikes.

Further information: www.east-greenland.com

IRELAND ~ LOUGH DERG:
SUSTAINABLE FOREST MANAGEMENT & TRADITIONAL SKILL BUILDING

BY ETAIN O'CARROLL

RICHARD CUMMINS LPI

WHEN TO GO

The volunteer projects run for two weeks and there are usually two projects between July and October. Check with SCI for exact dates.

GETTING THERE

You'll need to make your own way to Lough Derg. Flights into Galway and Shannon leave you a short bus journey away from Scariff in County Clare.

Food and accommodation are provided by CELT but you must pay a project fee to SCI (US$80 to US$130).

Conditions are basic: accommodation is in large tents, there is cold running water, and a compost toilet, but no electricity. Volunteers need to bring a sleeping bag, torch, work clothes, rain gear and gumboots.

If you'd rather not volunteer, two-day courses at weekend festivals cost US$145 and three-day courses are US$217.

D eep in the gorgeously green woods on the shore of Lough Derg in Ireland, local community group CELT (Centre for Environmental Living and Training) is quietly promoting environmental awareness and keeping Irish traditional skills alive.

The centre is dedicated to sustainable woodland management, education and training and runs a variety of workshops for schools and universities as well as adult training weekends. Two of the biggest events of the year are the Summer in the Woods and Weekend in the Woods festivals, where participants can learn everything from traditional herbal cures to canoe building, furniture making, dry-stone walling and natural building methods.

The festivals are very popular and volunteers are needed to help prepare for courses, run the weekends and assist with the clean-up afterwards. In return, volunteers get the opportunity to learn the skills being taught on the courses and meet a fascinating array of people. So if you've ever wanted to construct your own traditional round house, find a herbal cure for your aches and pains or get an introduction to silversmithing, woodcarving or longbow making, this could be the way to do it.

The volunteer projects are coordinated by Service Civil International (SCI), and although conditions are basic, it's a fantastic way to meet new friends and learn new skills. The projects do require some manual labour. With only a tent to retire to many participants find a hearty welcome in local village pubs where the renowned County Clare traditional music and dance scene is very much alive.

RESPONSIBLE TRAVEL CREDENTIALS

- CELT aims to increase environmental awareness through schools programmes, student exchanges and adult training courses.

- The organisation promotes the planting of native trees and the use of renewable energy.

- CELT aims to keep alive traditional skills such as basket weaving, dry-stone walling, canoe building and blacksmithing.

- CELT and SCI are not-for-profit organisations.

POLAND & BELARUS ~ BIAŁOWIEŻA:
BIOLOGISTS & BISON
BY JAMES JEFFREY

ADRIAN ARBIB | APL/CORBIS

Straddling the border between Poland and Belarus, the Białowieża primeval forest is the most important and largest remaining tract of the ancient lowland forest that covered Europe until 6000 years ago. At its heart, on the Polish side, lies the Białowieża National Park, a temperate wonderland of centuries-old trees, rare plants and an array of wildlife riches. Among them are 8500 insect species, 120 bird species, 11 species of amphibian and seven species of reptile. There are also 54 species of mammal including badger, lynx and wolf, but the most prominent of them is the European bison (auroch), which was wiped out here during WWI but reintroduced in 1929 and is now the symbol of the park. In 2005 local wildlife authorities opened a 20km walking trail with two viewing platforms to watch the bison do their stuff in their natural habitat.

Towering over them all are deciduous and evergreen tree species including ash, alder, hornbeam, lime, conifer, 50m spruce and ancient, moss-cloaked oak, some of which first popped out of their acorns when Shakespeare was still in short trousers. Close to 5000 hectares of the oldest part of the national park is designated as a special protection area.

The history of conservation in the area goes back a long way. Early protection was provided by Polish kings, Lithuanian princes and Russian tsars who were keen to have it preserved as a prime hunting ground. (Luftwaffe chief Hermann Göring entertained similar ideas when the area was under German occupation in WWII.) It was declared a National Reserve in 1921, added to the list of World Biosphere Reserves in 1977 and declared a Unesco World Heritage site in 1979. In 1996 the park area was almost doubled to 10,502 hectares.

Unfortunately, as the national park remains vulnerable to logging, the grand promises made by the Polish government to turn the entire forest into a national park have yet to turn into anything more solid.

RESPONSIBLE TRAVEL CREDENTIALS

- **From a natural point of view, this is one of the most important parks in Europe and is a magnet for biologists and conservationists. The national park's breeding centre for European bison is Poland's biggest.**

- **Tourism is only permitted in organised groups accompanied by licensed guides. In the Special Protection Area, hikers must stick to the paths to minimise disturbance.**

- **There are locally run tours that focus on the cultural aspects of the area. Tourism has encouraged the preservation of traditional architectural styles, such as houses with roofs constructed from reeds.**

- **Tourism to the park generates a lot of employment in the area for guides, accommodation providers, souvenir vendors and more. Any money spent here on local businesses and communities or with local guides helps to reduce dependence on farming and logging, both of which put pressure on the forest. The more money that is brought in by visitors keen to see the forest, the more it overturns logging company propaganda that expansion of the national park would be ruinous for the local economy.**

- **There is always the hope – hopefully not a misguided one – that the growing popularity of responsible tourism to Białowieża will persuade the Polish government to get its act together and fully protect the forest.**

WHEN TO GO

May to early October, neatly avoiding the mushy muckiness of early spring and the glum, muddy darkness of late autumn before the snow comes.

December to February for those hardier souls drawn by the austere beauty of winter.

GETTING THERE

Białowieża is 230km from Warsaw. There are regular trains (via Białystok) and buses, as well organised tours.

Accommodation options just outside the national park include camping, guesthouses, hotels and lots of B&Bs.

FACING PAGE: Białowieża is a last refuge for the European bison.

Climate Change, CO$_2$ & You

In recent years, cheap flights have opened up the skies and the furthest corners of the planet, enabling more travellers to fly further and more frequently than ever before. It's been a boon for many developing countries, where tourism (at least of the responsible variety!) has provided social and economic benefits to communities.

It's a great win for everyone, right? Well, not quite, when you consider the real cost of getting to those far-flung places.

Travelling by air has the highest environmental impact of any form of transport, as it chews up more carbon dioxide (CO$_2$) producing fossil fuels and spits out more water vapour and other heat-trapping gases than any other way of getting around. According to the Intergovernmental Panel on Climate Change, commercial aircraft already account for 3% to 4% of the total human impact on climate change – and it's growing.

For example, a return flight from London to New York produces 1.57 tonnes of CO$_2$, while Sydney to Bangkok pumps 2.1 tonnes of CO$_2$ into the atmosphere, according to www.climatecare.org.

Ironically, most credible sources agree that some of the world's most popular travel destinations will start to feel a significant impact from man-made climate change within the next few decades. Many argue it's already happening: glaciers are shrinking, ski seasons are shorter, and changing temperature and rainfall patterns are affecting wildlife and landscapes across the globe.

So what's a responsible traveller to do? There are a number of things you can do to reduce your personal energy use.

First up, you could stay home. Yeah, right. But you could consider staying *closer* to home. If you just want to fly and flop on a beach, do you really need to go to the other side of the planet to do it? How much exploring have you done in your own country?

Secondly, you can use other modes of transport: trains, buses, boats, kayaks, bicycles and walking are all viable options. And they're all good ways to connect with the world around you and to meet local people, without leaving much trace of your travels. Even if you fly to your destination, you can then take buses, for example, rather than internal flights.

The third option is to go carbon neutral. Several organisations – some charities, some businesses – will offset the emissions caused by your flight in exchange for a contribution to their cause. The carbon emissions from that London to New York flight, for example, can be offset with an investment of £10.18 at www.climatecare.org. Also check out the sites www.future forests.org and www.carbonneutral.com.au.

Tree planting is a staple activity of many carbon offsetting organisations. That said, some non-profits and other carbon-neutral organisations are starting to invest in sustainable and energy-saving projects in the developing world. Some of the most far-sighted initiatives offer employment to local people and conservation for their surrounding environments.

While being carbon neutral is an admirable goal, on a larger scale it might be seen as a way of making up for bad behaviour – a bit like dropping litter on a beautiful beach and then buying a bin to make up for it. That's why it's important to do more than think about – and hopefully support – a carbon-neutral initiative. Your style of travel can have a major impact on how 'friendly' your trip is to the environment.

Obviously, the actions of an individual are tiny next to the actions of governments and large corporations. Yet that doesn't mean we – individual travellers – should feel helpless. There's plenty we can do to minimise our impact on the environment. Going carbon neutral is a great place to start.

If you want to calculate how much carbon your next flight will emit, check out the CO$_2$ Air Travel Calculator at www.climatecare .org/airtravelcalc/airtravelcalc.cfm.

ROMANIA ~ CARPATHIAN MOUNTAINS:
BEAR SPOTTING IN TRANSYLVANIA
BY JOE CAWLEY

ERNEST MANEWAL, LPI

WHEN TO GO

WHEN TO GO

Romania's Carpathian Mountains have different personalities in winter and summer. Both are spectacular but, unsurprisingly, during the early winter hibernation period wildlife tracking may not be quite so fruitful.

GETTING THERE

There are many international flights to Bucharest. Zărneşti is a further three-hour drive from the capital.

Exodus Travel runs eight-day trips from August through March from A$1300 excluding flights.

Mention Transylvania and your first thoughts spring to a cloaked anaemic with problem dentistry, right? Well think again.

Think natural, not supernatural. Think alpine meadows, cuckoo calls and the largest concentration of large carnivores in Europe. Romania is where you're most likely to see wolves, bears and lynx, *au naturel*. Which brings me to why my backside was aching.

From within a potting-shed-on-legs deep in the southern Carpathian Mountains I had been shifting weight from buttock to buttock for over an hour in a stubborn determination to see a bear. In the cabin, Dan Marin, a local field guide, admitted that he hadn't spotted one since February. It was now May.

On the way to the lookout we came upon a hill-walker's heaven. A green baize stretched taut over rounded hills. Valleys carpeted with dark clusters of spruce and silver fir. Trails through meadows freckled with violet orchids and yellow broom. A million miles from the turbulent reputation of a country serially oppressed.

Carnivore tourism is shining just a sliver of light through the gloom of uncertainty and most of it originates from the Carpathian Large Carnivore Project (CLCP). Dan is one of ten local guides trained by the CLCP around which this particular Romanian wildlife adventure was based. The CLCP developed a ten-year conservation plan for large carnivores and their habitat incorporating a responsible-tourism programme to benefit the local population of Zărneşti, where the project is centred.

Along with most of the residents, Dan worked in the local munitions factory until a downturn in desire for Romanian weaponry forced a subtle career change. From a means of destruction to methods of conservation, under funding from the CLCP and the Department of Tourism, he learnt all there is to know about ambidextrous rodents and deciduous detective work.

As time plodded on, shards of dying sunlight sliced through the forest shade and it seemed that I was destined to remain unfulfilled. Then, about 35m away, a dark shadow shifted. The world fell silent for the king of the forest. With head bowed low it swaggered forwards on four huge pads. My mouth grew dry with a charge of adrenaline. Although our timber structure was sturdy, a determined bear weighing up to 320kg could reduce it to matchsticks within a matter of minutes.

Fortunately, this bear was not craving trekker treats. It stretched for a chunk of meat that members of the project had strung between two trees to enable sporadic monitoring, then nonchalantly padded up an embankment and disappeared behind a cloak of trees. Transylvania had finally revealed its true colours and Count Dracula was a teddy bear in comparison.

RESPONSIBLE TRAVEL CREDENTIALS

- **Projects such as this promote the ethic that man can live in harmony alongside large carnivores.**

- **The CLCP showed the local shepherds and residents that wolves and bears were worth more to them alive than dead. Now they're beginning to accept that conserving wildlife can bring an alternative revenue to their community.**

- **Trips such as these go some way towards helping to conserve endangered species and their habitat by donating part of the profits to conservation efforts.**

FACING PAGE: Romania has its own Big Five – European brown bear, wolf, lynx, deer and wild boar. The brown bear population is the largest outside Russia, but it's still on the threatened species list.

ROMANIA ~ DANUBE DELTA:
EUROPE'S UNSUNG WILDLIFE HAVEN
BY JAMES JEFFREY

At first glance the Romanian city of Tulcea looks like little more than a concrete ulcer blighting the banks of the Danube. But with its busy wharves and jostling ferries, it is the launching pad for voyages into one of the most extraordinary and far-flung corners of Europe: the Danube Delta.

Some 2860km from its origins in Germany's Black Forest, the Danube comes to an end so wild and isolated, it feels light years from the more polite upper reaches of the river that once had Strauss whipping himself into a frenzy of waltzes. As it approaches Romania's Black Sea coast and the edge of Europe, the river breaks into three main branches to form the continent's second-biggest delta (after the Volga), an environment of such variety and richness that Unesco was moved to declare it a Natural World Heritage site.

As you navigate the arms of the river and the channels that crisscross the Delta's 5640 sq km, passing traditional fishing villages that lie hours by boat from any road, you can encounter a proliferation of mammal and reptile life, 45 species of fish and 1150 species of plant. Add to that the gobsmacking drawcard of 300 species of bird; the Danube Delta is one of the world's most important breeding grounds for migratory birds.

This is also a wilderness of lakes convulsing with amorous frogs, reed isles, tropical woods, pastures, sand dunes, subtropical forests and, spreading over almost a quarter of a million hectares, one of the world's largest reed beds.

The former Romanian dictator Nicolae Ceauşescu, who never knowingly shied away from the idea of large-scale environmental vandalism, once had plans to tame the Delta and convert it into farmland to feed Communism's insatiable appetite for quota fulfilment. Thankfully, the old monster was thwarted before he was able to get too far, and these days Romania seems a lot keener on hanging on to its wild treasure.

Everyone needs a (relatively easily obtained) permit to enter the delta, which has been carefully divided by the nation's scientists into three categories of territory: areas where controlled fishing and hunting are permitted; areas where low impact, environmentally sensitive tourism can be developed; and areas, such as the 500-year-old Letea forest, which are closed to all human activity with the exception of scientists.

RESPONSIBLE TRAVEL CREDENTIALS

- **There are a number of Romanian operators offering tours of the Delta, and given that Romania is one of the most impoverished countries in Europe, any money you spend domestically is better than none. Some of the most specialised and intimate Delta touring is available directly through the villagers, fishermen and wildlife rangers who live in the Delta. Not only do you enjoy a richer experience, your tourist dollars go directly to a poor part of a poor country and reduce local dependence on hunting and fishing.**

- **The people of the Delta are hospitable (sometimes to the extent that you may have trouble walking after meals) and curious, not to mention deeply knowledgeable about the environment they and their ancestors have lived in harmony with for generations. They are your best key to understanding the Delta.**

- **As a Unesco Natural World Heritage site administered by the Danube Delta Biosphere Reserve Authority, the Danube Delta is environmentally policed. Access to sensitive areas is limited, most forms of transport are relatively low impact, there are no big, glitzy resorts and, once you leave Tulcea, there are almost no cars.**

WHEN TO GO

Spring – the migratory birds arrive relatively late in the Delta in comparison to more western parts of Europe. If you go from late May until early September pack the mosquito repellent.

GETTING THERE

Tulcea is 334km – a short flight or five hours by express train – from Bucharest. Ferries set out for the villages of the Delta on a regular basis.

Accommodation choices range from camping and rooms in the homes of villagers (negotiate with the locals when you arrive) to hotels in some of the larger settlements and an ecofriendly resort set up as, wait for it, a traditional fishing village.

RUSSIA ~ LAKE BAIKAL: ENCIRCLING THE WORLD'S DEEPEST LAKE

BY SIMON RICHMOND

Known as the Pearl of Siberia, Lake Baikal is the world's oldest and deepest lake. This crystal clear lake, 636km long, 80km wide and 1637m deep near its western edge, contains nearly one-fifth of the globe's fresh water. Over 1000 species of animals and plants (most endemic) live in the lake, including the nerpa, the world's only freshwater seal. It is, quite rightly, the biggest tourist attraction in all of Siberia.

Most of the lake remains as pristine and beautiful as it was when it was formed some 25 million years ago, although it hasn't escaped modern-day pollution entirely. Most notoriously at its southern tip a paper and pulp plant has been dumping effluent into the lake since the 1960s. There are now fears that the northern end of the lake could be even worse affected by the construction of an oil pipeline.

Since the 1990s local environmental groups have been working with the US-based Earth Island Institute on the Baikal Watch project to help conserve and restore the area's native flora and fauna. One of the ways this is being done is through the construction of the Great Baikal Trail, a hiking trail around the entire lake that will link up the trails and tourist facilities that currently exist in the three national parks and four nature reserves that already protect some two-thirds of Baikal's shoreline. The grand plan is to eventually stretch the trail as far as the Mongolian border.

Less than a quarter of the planned 2000km of trail has so far been built. Each summer groups of tourist volunteers can take part in a range of locally organised construction and maintenance programmes around the lake, each chipping away at the mammoth task. All you need do is apply through either of the websites listed below and get yourself out there.

SIMON RICHMOND | LPI

RESPONSIBLE TRAVEL CREDENTIALS

- **Volunteer groups living and working on-site number between 15 and 20 people – the aim being to have half Russian and half international visitors.**

- **The trail's construction will allow continuous environmental monitoring of the lake and its shoreline. It will also help the local economy develop along responsible tourism lines; and it will provide environmental education for children and adults, as well as creating an opportunity for cultural exchange.**

- **The Great Baikal Trail is a grass-roots operation run by local and international environmentalist and volunteer citizens. Baikal Watch is a non-profit organisation.**

WHEN TO GO

Between May and August each year volunteers can take part in some 30-odd projects along the proposed course of the trail, each lasting between two and six weeks.

GETTING THERE

The nearest city to Lake Baikal is Irkutsk, which has international flight connections and is also on the Trans-Siberian Railway.

During projects, transport, meals and accommodation are provided free of charge. Accommodation is either in tents or basic log cabins within the park areas or along the proposed route of the trail.

Volunteers have to bring their own sleeping bag, ground mat and all-weather clothing.

SWITZERLAND ~ WENGEN: TIPTOE THROUGH ALPINE FLOWERS

BY ADAM LONG

If you're looking to go where no man has gone before, then a comfortable, family-run hotel in Wengen is probably not for you. If, however, you'd like to explore Switzerland's most outrageously over-the-top chocolate box scenery (and thoroughly acquaint yourself with the contents of said chocolate box at the same time) then a week in this idyllic alpine resort nestled in the hills above Interlaken will be just your cup of cocoa.

The wildflower-fest begins each day after a hearty breakfast (at a civilised hour) to fuel you for a not-too-rugged day of hiking. A well-known British naturalist type, David Tattersfield, leads the way through meadows carpeted with such treasures as the bearded bellflower and (if you're lucky) the rare lady slipper orchid. The less botanically obsessed walker, who might eventually grow tired of the creeping azaleas your expert guide points out, need only lift their eyes (up and up and up) to see those three majestic show-offs, the Eiger, the Jungfrau and the Mönch.

There's a different peak towering overhead each day, perhaps with ibex and chamois grazing the steep slopes, or even an avalanche to watch on the distant heights. Butterfly-lovers and bird-watchers won't be disappointed either, as your trail carries you across glacier-fed streams and through open forests of spruce. If your strength begins to fail you, despite regularly administered doses of fine chocolate, there's often the option of a train ride home at the end of a long day.

DOMINIC ARIZONA BONUCCELLI | LPI

RESPONSIBLE TRAVEL CREDENTIALS

- **For 150 years or more, well-to-do European adventurers have been coming to this region for the views, the air and the exercise. Now, as then, you rely on your own two feet to get about, or the quaint cog railways (with the option of a cable car here and there), so it serves as a long-established model for responsible tourism, rather than an environment under threat.**

- **Cuckoo clock anyone? If a village of perfect gingerbread chalets is a cliché, it's still a traditional community, albeit one dressed up for the tourist trade.**

- **Not all your hard-earned will end up in a vault in Zurich; you'll stay and eat in the family-run Hotel Berghaus (on the edge of the village, with views to make your eyes spin).**

WHEN TO GO

Tours are timed for late June to coincide with the best floral displays.

GETTING THERE

By train from Zurich, or take a connecting flight from London.

Change trains twice (at Bern and Interlaken) on the way to Lauterbrunnen, before a steep and spectacular funicular ride to Wengen.

Your base, the Berghaus Hotel, is five minutes' walk from the station. Don't worry, you'll get plenty of exercise in the next week; the hills are alive with the sound of hiking boots for eight hours a day – though you'll only need to be moderately fit as there will be time to potter about and smell the flowers.

Naturetrek's Wengen – Alpine Flowers of the Swiss Alps tour costs £1095 (London to London) all inclusive, for eight days or £975 (Zurich to Zurich).

Further information: www.naturetrek.co.uk

Take a Hike on the Cheap

BY KERRYN BURGESS

Weekend newspapers are full of tempting ads for three-week guided hiking trips in fabulous places on the other side of the world. Average cost? A good chunk of annual salary if you add on airfares, spending money, single supplements, tips, currency exchange fees and disappointing lunches. Not to mention fossil-fuel use that'd make a Texan oil baron rub his greasy palms together in glee.

The alternative? Virtually free, all-organised, conservation-minded, fun, close to home. I've had it hiking and canoeing along the languid brown waters of South Australia's Lower Glenelg River, a thin strip of national park where pelicans bob around like bath toys. Living in Canada, I've had it swimming in the clear, cold depths of the Bruce Peninsula, part of a Unesco World Biosphere Reserve. I've had it hiking in Ontario's Killarney Provincial Park, where I once ate breakfast across the lake from a moose. Your ticket: membership of a hiking club.

Hiking club membership typically provides guided access to conservation areas within weekend distance of home. Expect regular organised trips, car-pooling, and advice on gear, food and fitness, all for less than US$100 per year, plus minimal expenses.

This year I led a club trip to Australia's Dandenong Ranges National Park, about an hour by train from central Melbourne. In a day of walking through tall mountain ash forests, lush ferns and pin-up waterfalls, the only other hikers my group encountered were a group of Japanese tourists hoping to see koalas. It seemed more of Melbourne's population was drinking tea in the Himalaya or trudging behind a porter on the Inca Trail than hiking close to home. True, I didn't get to email my mates from an Internet café in Kathmandu afterwards, but it was wild and beautiful, and I got there for the price of a train ticket.

The trick is to find a club that suits your age and interests. If 'alpine' appears in the name, expect a lot of hard-core expeditioners. In most countries (but not the UK), clubs with 'ramblers' in the name tend to be aimed at seniors. Clubs for gay and lesbian hikers are invariably called 'Out and About'. Some clubs attract a lot of families, while others virtually double as dating agencies. Most are happy for nonmembers to come along on at least one trip before signing up, and this is a good opportunity to check out the club's vibe as well as its official policies.

Trips are usually advertised well in advance via a club newsletter or website – next weekend I'm off snow-shoeing in Australia's Alpine National Park. My club was instrumental in persuading the state government to ban cattle grazing from this park, and a campaign for World Heritage listing is gathering momentum as a result.

CHOOSING A CLUB

- **Stay close to home to minimise fossil-fuel use, and look for a club with a minimal-impact hiking policy. This might mean using public transport or car-pooling, limiting group size, selecting routes carefully, going smelly (no soap), rugging up (no camp fires), taking only photos (not souvenirs) and leaving only footprints (not rubbish).**

- **Look for a club that actively pressures governments and businesses to be environmentally responsible and conserve sensitive areas. Then get active! Campaign activity and club membership are great ways to build communities.**

- **On a global level, an economy reliant on fossil fuels is unsustainable. On a personal and local level, club membership is inexpensive, leaving you more money to donate to conservation campaigns in your area.**

For further information see the club listings on these websites:
Australia: www.outdooraustralia.com /clubspgs/clublink.htm
Canada: www.mec.ca
New Zealand: www.fmc.org.nz
UK: www.ramblers.org.uk
USA: www.webwalking.com/hike.shtml

North America

CANADA ~ ARCTIC CIRCLE:
SUNRISE CELEBRATIONS & SLED DOGS

BY ETAIN O'CARROLL

ALISON WRIGHT | LPI

Restless throughout the college year and immediately off hitchhiking around Europe as soon as the summer holidays began, I knew I needed one last trip to settle me down before getting a job. I applied to Frontiers Foundation, a Canadian organisation working with First Nations and Inuit, for a place on a three-month volunteer project. I'd long been fascinated by Native American culture and was delighted when they took me on. It was almost three years later when I came home, and even then I was reluctant to do so.

Those first three months were spent on a tiny, remote reserve north of Lake Superior. Well off the highway, down a dirt track rippled like a washboard, the clutter of shabby houses, dogs and old cars became home while I worked on construction projects for low-income families. Like most native communities this one struggled to cope with severe social problems and although it was kilometres from anywhere in many ways it resembled the toughest inner-city neighbourhoods.

In an attempt to counteract some of these problems and improve life on the reserve, traditional healing ceremonies were being revived. Very few outsiders ever made it onto tribal land (the children wondered if I could 'see the same' with my green eyes) and I was privileged to be invited to take part. Sweat lodges, full-moon circles and celebrations of the sunrise soon became a part of my life.

No amount of money, no executive placement and no holiday company could ever have bought me the experiences I had. It was incredibly humbling and profoundly important to me that I had been accepted by the community in this way. When the project came to an end the thought of returning to Ireland to work in advertising seemed so crass that I just couldn't do it.

In January of the following year I was transferred to an education project in a small town 480km north of the Arctic Circle. I landed in the pitch dark in mid-afternoon and almost choked as I took my first breath of thermometer-challenging Arctic air.

Over the next two years I worked in two different communities, in schools and adult education colleges, helping out wherever I could, tutoring everything from basic literacy skills to desktop publishing. The lower the temperature, the worse the blizzard, and the more extreme the environment, the more I loved it. I was totally smitten.

Working with the schools and making friends with local hunters I was given the opportunity to spend a lot of time 'on the land'. Camping on frozen lakes, watching herds of musk ox or caribou meandering over the hills, and seeing the snow and ice being carved into beautiful angular shapes I always expected the hushed tones of a commentary by David Attenborough to begin. Life became a series of events I never, in my wildest dreams, thought I would experience.

Years later I still crave to go north, I miss the sense of adventure and I miss the sense of community you get in a tiny village that has no road access and only has a plane arrive twice a week. It was difficult to finally come home and for years after I toyed with going back. I may have worked for free but money couldn't have bought what were some of the most fascinating and rewarding years of my life.

RESPONSIBLE TRAVEL CREDENTIALS

• **You'll be living in the local community, exchanging knowledge and assistance that benefit everyone involved.**

WHEN TO GO

Projects begin from June to September each year.

Construction projects begin in June, July and August and require a three-month commitment.

A 10-month (September to June) commitment is required for volunteers on education projects.

GETTING THERE

Housing construction and renovation projects take place across the north of Canada, with about half being above the Arctic Circle.

Volunteers should have some experience in construction or a related trade.

Most of the education projects involve volunteers working in schools in the Northwest Territories, Nunavut and the Yukon.

Although Frontiers considers all applications, it helps to have some teaching or tutoring experience when applying for these positions.

Volunteers must be at least 18 years old.

CANADA ~ JOHNSTONE STRAIT:
ORCA WATCHING AT WATER LEVEL
BY KERRY LORIMER & RACHEL ALT

MICHAEL LAANELA LPI

WHEN TO GO

Viewing season is from the end of April until the end of October.

GETTING THERE

Vancouver Island is accessible by ferry or flight from Washington State or British Colombia. Pacific Northwest Adventures has three- and six-day kayaking expeditions departing from Port McNeill, on the northeastern end of Vancouver Island. They depart every Tuesday (three days, C$1695) and Sunday (six days, C$1493) between June and September, including all meals. All kayaking and group camping equipment is provided. Tents and sleeping bags are not provided but may be hired for a nominal fee.

No previous kayaking experience is necessary and you need only moderate fitness.

Seeing a 2m dorsal fin slice past less than 15m from your kayak is a butt-clenching, gob-stopping experience – and the signal to raft up with your fellow kayakers to play the part of unobtrusive observers to one of the ocean's most efficient predators: the orca. In the quiet of a deserted cove, the sounds of the orcas splashing and blowing are amplified and, with kayakers seen as more of a curiosity than a threat, the whales go about their fun unperturbed.

Each summer, around 100 orcas follow migrating schools of salmon down the coast of British Columbia to Johnstone Strait, the narrow strip of sea between Vancouver Island and the mainland. There, they hang out for the summer, feeding, rubbing their bellies clean on pebble beaches and socialising.

More than 20 companies operate whale-watching tours around Vancouver Island, and as many as 40 vessels keep each pod company – it can feel a bit crowded, even when everyone observes legal observation rules.

Watching from water level, from a small and silent craft – ie a sea kayak – is a wildlife experience on the whales' terms. It's not unusual for them to approach quite close. And not just the orcas: the Strait and surrounds are haven to a range of cetaceans including humpback whales, Dall's porpoises and Pacific white-sided dolphins.

Locally owned operator Pacific Northwest Expeditions has a strong focus on education and conservation. Guides give a natural history interpretation of the whales, as well as of the marine and terrestrial environments. They will also help you to identify individual whales by their distinctive markings and let you eavesdrop on their underwater 'conversations' via a hydro-phone.

You can do day tours to see the whales, but if you camp or stay in a waterside or floating lodge, or aboard a yacht, you're there when the day-trippers have gone. You can enjoy the area's stunning natural beauty – the Strait runs between the rainforest of Vancouver Island and the white-capped peaks of mainland British Colombia's coastal range. And, as you stand amid the serenity you can, with luck, reflect on the feeling of coming face to face with a five-tonne killer.

RESPONSIBLE TRAVEL CREDENTIALS

- **Local regulatory organisations like the Whale Watch Operations Association Northwest (WWOAN) restrict watercraft of any size from getting closer than 100m to the orcas, and most tour operators stay within that boundary. Paddling a sea kayak is the least obtrusive way to watch whales.**

- **Johnstone Strait and Blackfish Bay are the traditional territory of the Namgis and the Mamalilikulla-Qwe'Qwa'Sot'Em First Nations people. Pacific Northwest Expeditions consults with them regarding tourism activities on an ongoing basis.**

- **A portion of the company's revenue goes towards wild orca research in British Colombia, and the company is directly involved in consultative development of regulations to protect local marine mammals.**

FACING PAGE: Male orcas (on the left) can be distinguished from females by the height of their dorsal fin – up to 2m tall.

CANADA ~ SASKATCHEWAN:
SADDLE SORES & SPIRITUAL LORE
BY ADAM LONG

MARK NEWMAN | LPI

PHOTOLIBRARY

WHEN TO GO

This is Canada – don't go in the winter!

GETTING THERE

The Two Worlds of the Horse tour costs C$2460 for nine days, per person, all-inclusive, departing Regina.

With the Cree you sleep in a tepee, on the ranch in a cabin. It's basic but comfortable.

After a long day in the saddle, try lying back in a tepee watching the smoke from your camp-fire spiral towards the stars twinkling in the narrow opening above… and see if *that* doesn't bring you closer to understanding the mysteries of the universe! The night sky doesn't come any wider nor the stars any brighter than on the prairies of Saskatchewan, and you may even get to see the northern lights as well.

Way out west of Regina, the Saskatchewan state capital, Great Excursions offers a nine-day experience of frontier horse-riding, with the chance to play at being both cowboys *and* Indians. The horse has been the common denominator for both First Nations and European settlers, and this trip aims to give you an understanding of the history and culture of both. For the first few days you live with a Cree Indian family, Hugh and Barbara Lerat, in the beautiful Qu'Appelle Valley. The Lerats will gladly share as much of their spiritual lore and traditional healing skills as you care to learn, all while sailing on horseback across an endless sea of grassland or around the evening camp fire.

This is also the land of the Mountie, and you visit a museum dedicated to those square-jawed men in funny hats and even funnier pants en route to a ranch in the formidable Cypress Hills.

Here, where the plains meet the tall timber of the high country, you'll sit high in the saddle and wear your plaid shirt with pride, ride lonesome trails and round up cattle, help mend fences and even hear some cowboy poetry, courtesy of host Scott Reesor whose family has operated the Reesor ranch – a working cattle ranch (as opposed to a 'guest' ranch) – for generations.

Before you wander bow-legged back to civilisation you'll have lived and breathed two distinct local histories and cultures.

RESPONSIBLE TRAVEL CREDENTIALS

- You'll see plenty of wildlife, and learn how two very different peoples share (and impact upon) the same ecosystem.

- By sharing their traditional knowledge with tourists, First Nation Elders can afford to bring Indigenous kids from the city out to the plains to get a taste of the old ways, and instil a bit of pride about who they are.

- Your hosts are all local families, and the success of their businesses keeps alive not only the Indian culture but the cowboy way of life threatened by modern industrial agri-business. Great Excursions aims to deliver an emotionally stimulating experience for travellers with hungry minds.

FACING PAGE: Elk scrabble for green shoots through a light dusting of snow. Winter gets chilly, but summer temperatures range from 10°C to 25°C.

Further information: www.greatexcursions.com

LOW-IMPACT CAMPING AMONG ANASAZI RUINS
BY RAY BARTLETT

ERNEST MANEWAL LPI

The sunrise on the way to Bluff, Utah, sets the tone: morning light on the giant red monoliths of stone make them look like sailing ships on a strange, deserted ocean. I'm suddenly excited: a week in a river-carved canyon, using llamas to carry our tents and gear. To my surprise, leading a llama is easy, even fun.

We ford a stream and meander through wind-carved cottonwoods, impenetrable thickets of tamarisk, overlooks of pink sandstone and cholla cactus. It is April, and the fishhook barrel cacti are starting to bloom: bright fuchsia splashes on an otherwise muted landscape. My wife notices a ruin tucked beneath the overhanging ledge on the opposite canyon wall. The Anasazi, a cliff-dwelling native culture of hunter-gatherers that disappeared about 700 years ago, have left their mark all throughout the American Southwest.

Suddenly, there's commotion on the trail. 'Kiyah! Kiyah!' a man calls out, and four men on horseback gallop through the arroyo, churning up clouds of dust and tearing up the trail. Breaking branches as they push through the riverbed, they head over to the ruin we'd spotted on the opposite cliff. They dismount briefly, take some pictures, then remount and – hooting and hollering – gallop further up into the canyon.

The painted pinks and pastel hues of the desert seem almost normal as we near the end of the trip. After a week of hikes up into Fish Canyon's slot canyons, poking around Anasazi ruins, and looking down from scenic vistas, we have found all we were looking for: arrowhead flakes, a corn grinding stone, and even pottery shards with an intricate printed design.

RESPONSIBLE TRAVEL CREDENTIALS

- **Llamas leave – literally – a much smaller footprint on the ecology of the desert than horses or burros. With split toes instead of hooves, they cause less damage to fragile soils and plants. They're quiet, their droppings are more like a native deer's than a horse's and they rarely stop to chomp grasses or vegetation. They also make it easy to pack out what you pack in. And while it's tempting to take home souvenir shards or arrowhead flakes, everything discovered is left where it was found.**

WHEN TO GO

March, April and May have the best flowers and the most available water – by August the riverbeds are totally dry.

GETTING THERE

Flying directly into Bluff is possible, but prohibitively expensive. Albuquerque or Santa Fe are closest; from there rent a car. It's a beautiful five-hour drive, and – timed right – you can catch Monument Valley as well.

Llamas are pack animals only, not for riding (although they 'heel' far more naturally than horses). You'll need to be fit enough to hike several kilometres per day. Be sure to bring sunscreen, plenty of water, maps and GPS, and a purification system.

Prices vary substantially depending on groups' needs: non-guided tours (you take care of the llama yourself) are US$50 per day for one llama or US$40 per animal per day for two or more. Guided trips start at US$300 per person per day and drop to US$250 per person per day for four to six people. A guide/handler can be added to any trip for US$100 to US$150 per day. A tent is included in the price along with other 'communal' gear, but guests are expected to have their own sleeping bag, pad and day pack.

Wilderness Wanderings: How to Minimise your Impact on Fragile Places

No matter what you do, your mere presence will make some impact on any given environment – the trick is to keep that impact short term and minimal. Occasionally, a wilderness area may be deemed so fragile that prudence warrants it being left altogether untouched and untravelled.

Here are some tips for the trail to minimise your personal footprint, which can apply equally as well to remote wilderness as to parkland in your own backyard.

HIKING

- Keep erosion to a minimum: don't be tempted to create a new track or take a shortcut. Stay on the existing trail where possible, even if it's muddy or there's room to walk alongside.

- While you're admiring the view, try to keep one eye on your feet! Particularly at high altitudes and latitudes, native flora can be very slow growing. It can take years to regenerate after being crushed by your clod-hopper. If you have to traverse an area of delicate wildflowers, grasses or mosses, keep to the outskirts and aim to step on rocks and compacted soil rather than plants.

- Whatever you schlep in, you should schlep out – if it can't be properly disposed of along the way. Many developing countries, in particular, lack adequate services to dispose of your rubbish. This includes plastic and food scraps, batteries and those ubiquitous cigarette butts. Take an empty film canister as an ashtray, and a plastic bag to collect your rubbish along the way. Go one step further and pick up litter you see along the trail. Dispose of your trash responsibly: think about where it will end up.

- Take a strong water bottle and boil or purify your drinking water, rather than buying bottled water: the scourge of the 21st century is shaping up to be discarded plastic water bottles.

CAMPING

- If you're in a sensitive area, select sandy or non-vegetated surfaces (or leaf litter) to pitch your tent: although that alpine meadow looks enticing, you could be doing irreparable damage to delicate flora. In the interests of further minimising erosion, don't dig drainage ditches around your tent.

- Set your tent up at least 30m away from a lake or watercourse. This ensures you don't pollute the stream, and don't cut off access to the water source for wildlife (in the event of a flash flood, you also stand a better chance of not being washed away!).

TOILET HYGIENE

- Tent pegs make good shovels: if you get caught short on the trekking trail, dig a hole at least 15cm deep (or 30cm in hot areas), on the lower side of the trail, preferably at least 100m from it.

- Take a cigarette lighter and burn your toilet paper. If there is a risk of fire, or the ground is too hard or stony to dig a hole, use leaf litter or rocks to cover.

- Make sure you're at least 100m away from any watercourse.

- Don't dispose of tampons etc along the trail – native animals are very good at digging up and scattering buried rubbish. Carry a small plastic bag and dispose of them responsibly.

WASHING & WATER POLLUTION

- Pack biodegradable soaps and shampoos that don't contain phosphates, and don't use them directly in fresh waterways – use a bowl or bottle and lather up and rinse 50m from the water's edge.

- The same applies for washing pots and pans: elbow grease is a good alternative to excess soap.

- If bathing or swimming, consider the sensibilities of local people – both regarding what you wear and using 'their' water. Bathe downstream from water collection points or villages.

CAMP FIRES

- Before you light up, check if fires are permitted (or even sensible) – either from a safety or an environmental perspective.

- Try to use an existing site. Check for overhanging foliage and clear the area around the fire of any potential fire hazards.

- Use only dead timber from fallen trees: standing trees, even dead ones, provide important habitat for wildlife.

- Keep your fire as small as possible – don't flagrantly waste wood (particularly if local people are also relying on it).

- Don't throw non-biodegradable material into the fire – particularly batteries and plastic.

- Never leave a fire unattended and keep some water handy in case it gets out of control. Make sure all embers are extinguished and try to leave the site with as little obvious disturbance as possible.

USA ~ GRAND CANYON:
A WINTER'S TALE
BY SAM BENSON

CURTIS MARTIN | LPI

RICHARD CUMMINS LPI

You can't savour the verdant valleys of Yosemite or the mountain peaks of Yellowstone in a throng of thousands. So, what's the solution? It's a matter of timing: visit in the off-season and you'll have glorious national parks such as the Grand Canyon almost all to yourself.

There are amazing experiences you can only have if you visit America's iconic Grand Canyon in the off-season. In winter, there's no jostling at canyon overlooks and almost no helicopters or planes buzzing overhead to disrupt your contemplations. On the canyon's north rim, you can ski in and snow-camp where (blissfully) no cars are allowed.

Back on the south rim, you can snow-shoe on canyon rim trails or cross-country ski in the surrounding Kaibab National Forest. The unpredictable winter weather is dramatic, too: canyons filled with clouds, sunshine sparkling on snow like diamonds, and crisp, cool nights perfect for star-gazing and curling up around a crackling fireplace.

Peak season at the Grand Canyon runs from Memorial Day (last Monday in May) to Labor Day (first Monday in September), when more than 20,000 tourists enter the park daily, as compared with just over 25% of that in February. Almost all of the activities that happen at the Grand Canyon during summer (except river rafting) continue in winter, weather permitting.

You can take a mule ride or make the rugged trek (with poles and crampons) down to the canyon floor and overnight at rustic Phantom Ranch, where average daily highs may reach 15°C to 20°C even mid-winter. With a four-wheel drive vehicle, it's possible to drive Diamond Creek Rd from Peach Springs on the Hualapai Reservation down to the Colorado River via a side canyon year-round.

These days, America's national parks are being loved to death. As more Americans travel in their own backyards, and international tourists are increasingly drawn to the USA's great wild places, these wide-open spaces are in danger of becoming just parking lots with views. Don't fight the crowds – leave them behind all winter long.

RESPONSIBLE TRAVEL CREDENTIALS

- **Visiting a US national park in the off-season helps alleviate the strain on natural resources and the environmental impact of overcrowding and development.**

- **Because so few people visit the Grand Canyon in winter, you'll have a more personalised and rewarding national park experience, thanks to less-harried park staff.**

- **National park gateway towns rely on peak-season tourist receipts to make it through the year, so an off-season vacation supports independent local businesses.**

WHEN TO GO

The south rim is open all year. The north rim is open mid-May to mid-October; you can drive in and camp until snow closes the road from Jacob Lake (usually by mid-November) or ski in anytime after that (backcountry permit required).

GETTING THERE

From Las Vegas you can pick up a rental car (from US$35 per day) or board a commuter or tourist flight to Tusayan (from US$100), near the south rim.

If you're driving, you can drop your car in Williams (Arizona) and board the vintage Grand Canyon Railway (www.thetraincom; round-trip adult/child US$75/40) to Grand Canyon Village on the south rim.

Free shuttle buses on the south rim operate to major points of interest and trail-heads year-round, except along the Hermits Rest route (March to November only), which remains open to private vehicles between December and February.

Reserve lodge rooms and mule rides through Xanterra Parks & Resorts (www.grandcanyonlodges.com) in advance.

Further information: www.nps.gov/grca

USA ~ MAINE COAST:
SAILING A HISTORIC WINDJAMMER
BY ALEX LEVITON

WHEN TO GO

Depending on the windjammer, trips run anywhere from late May to mid-October. Expect a bit of rain and chilly nights, especially in the shoulder season.

GETTING THERE

Fly into either Portland, Maine or Boston (Massachusetts) and take a train or bus (or Windjammer van service from Portland) to the Camden and Rockland area where the ships depart.

Fourteen windjammer tall ships hold from six to 40 people in single, double and triple cabins. Book well in advance for special weeks featuring photography, windjammer races or singing. Prices are around US$110 per person per day, including food, lodging and the last night's lobster bake.

After the first night pitching and rolling in gale-force winds, I awoke at 7am to the sound of activity. The rare summer storm was over and on deck coffee was brewing, breakfast was cooking on the cast-iron stove, and my initiation as salty seadog was about to begin. I was spending a week on the 1922 oyster-dredger-turned-passenger sailing vessel, the *J & E Riggin*.

The first job I volunteered for was bringing up the anchor. You don't get much more authentic than the *Riggin* – no on-board motor, just a diesel yawl (dinghy) to ease the ship into dock if needs be. That means the anchor is cranked in by hand by people, I found out soon enough, much, much stronger than me. So I transferred to flaking the chain. Ah, yes, of course…flaking the chain, I thought. Now this sounded like a seafaring mission. It turns out flaking the chain involves de-kinking an anchor chain that has just spent a night in 3m of ocean-floor muck. My hands were the first part of me to look the part of seadog.

By day we sailed the dramatic Maine coast, by night we anchored in peaceful coves. To compensate for our hardy workouts, we ate as I'd imagined old swabbies would eat. Or, perhaps, culturally sensitive, organic swabbies. Captain Annie, wife of Captain John, doubled as chef and gardener, and added her practically golf ball–sized blueberries she'd picked just days before to our organic pancakes. Meals were on deck, buffet style and all homemade: clam chowder (New England, of course) for lunch, chilli and cornbread for dinner. While we ate dinner one night, the deckhands entertained us with the hip-hop version of 'Blow the Man Down'.

Since that voyage, I've been sailing a few times. I still have to say to myself, 'Port has four letters and so does left. Port equals left, starboard equals right.' But every time I get a whiff of salt water, I smile knowingly.

PHOTOLIBRARY

RESPONSIBLE TRAVEL CREDENTIALS

- The 14 windjammers in the fleet all have a 'leave-no-trace' policy. The vessels rely almost solely on wind and tide (read: don't bring a hairdryer). Dishes are often washed in sea water using biodegradable soap.

- The windjammers and their staff keep the sailing traditions alive, singing sea shanties and regaling passengers with stories. The fleet is the largest collection of commercial sailing vessels left in the US, dating back to 1871.

- Each windjammer is privately owned by long-time Maine residents and uses as much local produce as possible, much of it organically grown. Six vessels have produced their own cookbooks.

USA ~ ROUTE 66:
ROAD TRIPPIN'
BY SAM BENSON

JOHN NEUBAUER LPI

The iconic American road trip is Route 66. It first connected the prairie capital of Chicago with the orange groves outside Los Angeles in the 1920s. What John Steinbeck called the 'Mother Road' also gave birth to the classic American driving vacation, starting in the 1950s. It was eventually bypassed by the interstate system, modelled after Germany's autobahn. So, today the Mother Road exists in a parallel universe of nostalgic highways and gravel roads.

I'd dreamed of driving its 3550km ever since I'd moved to California. Starting at Santa Monica Pier down by the Pacific Ocean, I gunned my car's engine and whooped as I sped down the road. Only to learn, as I crawled through the endless suburbs of LA, that Route 66 is actually a crash course in the soul-satisfying 'slow travel' movement.

Though the goal of tourists is usually to get from point A to point B as quickly as possible, driving the 'Main Street of America' takes time. Even just finding the old highway can be a puzzle in places, making me feel like a kid on a treasure hunt. Happily, I got lost a lot. Detours to oddball attractions such as the Exotic World Burlesque Museum & Striptease Hall of Fame in the Mojave Desert or the Old West town of Oatman, where they literally fry eggs on the sidewalk on the 4th of July, were irresistible – and unforgettable.

In big cities like St Louis and Albuquerque, following old Route 66 led me to phenomenal diners and cowboy steakhouses I'd have missed if I'd just stayed on the boring interstate. Then there were those unspoiled spots I stumbled across and virtually had all to myself, like sunset over the Painted Desert and the golden Oklahoma prairies outside Tulsa.

Most of the family-run pit stops along Route 66 were open shorter hours, so I found myself only covering about 160km each day before I pulled into a vintage 1930s motor court, gossiped over dinner at the local diner, and then kicked back with a cold beer under the stars.

By the time I rolled into my hometown in Illinois, my digital camera was full of photos of places no-one else I knew had ever seen and of all the eccentrics, iconoclasts and pioneers I'd chewed the fat with en route. My bags were full of kitschy, cool souvenirs, and I was addicted to getting my kicks on Route 66, the slower, old-fashioned way.

RESPONSIBLE TRAVEL CREDENTIALS

- Driving off the interstate at lower speeds and for fewer kilometres per day impacts the ozone layer less than most road trips. Cycling and using public transport as much as possible to explore local areas of interest further cuts down on air pollution.

- Route 66 connects hundreds of small towns, where you'll get to meet and interact with locals, as well as encounter living social history, especially in Native America.

- You'll spend your vacation dollars at mom-and-pop motels and diners instead of multinational chains, and support historic preservation efforts just by patronising local attractions along the route. Without tourism, many of these places wouldn't even exist.

WHEN TO GO

If you're driving east to west, a late summer/early autumn trip is best, as the peak-season crush will be over and the deserts will have cooled off by the time you arrive. In the reverse direction, starting out in late spring avoids cold weather and snowy roads back east.

GETTING THERE

Start in Chicago or Santa Monica, a city next to Los Angeles. There are international and domestic flights to O'Hare and LAX airports, respectively.

One-way car rentals can be expensive (US$500 return fee), but will save you (and the environment) the trouble of driving back to where you started from.

If you're driving your own car, make sure you have a roadside assistance plan. A four-wheel drive isn't necessary, but some sections of Route 66 can be in rough condition.

Motorcycles use less petrol and are great on Route 66, as long as you're an experienced driver.

USA ~ SIERRA CLUB:
EPIC HIKE & HELPING HANDS
BY SAM BENSON

By taking a volunteer holiday with the Sierra Club, you can dare to take the epic American hikes you've always dreamed of and, at the same time, save them for future travellers. Sierra Club trips often let you access places that the general public can't go, which lets you experience the rare tranquillity of untouched American parklands.

With the Sierra Club, you can maintain alpine trails in Glacier National Park, replant forests along the north rim of the Grand Canyon or wander in the sand-dune habitats of Cape Cod National Seashore. Even if you're not a landlubber, some volunteer holidays combine hiking with kayak or canoe trails, such as rafting through the spectacular canyons of the Green River at Utah's Dinosaur National Monument. Best of all, you'll have more fun than if you did it on your own, since the Sierra Club group camaraderie is unbeatable.

Wherever you go and whatever trails you work on, you'll get more out of your Sierra Club volunteer holiday than you have to give. For beginners, these trips are perfect for practising Wilderness Skills 101, with the safety net of an experienced group leader to guide you – at no extra cost. What's more, Sierra Club outings are often accompanied by local field experts, so you'll get more out of your trip into the great outdoors than you would by yourself or while being herded around on an expensive, large-group organised tour.

If you've got a passion for hiking, you'll know that each step you take along a trail brings it that much closer to crumbling. Millions of footsteps across America each year, from the Rocky Mountains to the Appalachians, wear away the very paths that bring hikers into all of that natural grandeur. But does that mean you have to hang up your hiking shoes? No way. Try a Sierra Club trip, and you'll be hooked on the feel-good, do-good factor too.

WADE EAKLE | LPI

RESPONSIBLE TRAVEL CREDENTIALS

- Sierra Club volunteer holidays help preserve trails and restore ecosystems.

- You'll meet small groups of like-minded folks who enjoy the same activities, plus get a unique opportunity to learn *in situ* with scientists, naturalists and other field educators.

- Each year Sierra Club volunteers donate about 27,000 hours (worth nearly a half million dollars) to federal and state parks, preserves, and wilderness and wildlife refuges.

WHEN TO GO

The Sierra Club offers volunteer holidays year-round, with more opportunities in summer. Sign up as far in advance as possible, as trips can fill quickly.

GETTING THERE

Sierra Club volunteer holidays typically cost from US$395 for a one-week trip. Annual membership costs from US$25. Being fairly fit is essential; prior outdoors experience is helpful, but not necessary.

To sign up for a trip you'll need to fill out a questionnaire for approval by the group leader, sign a liability release form and buy your own travel insurance.

Participants are responsible for arranging their own transportation to the meeting point, from where shared transportation is provided to the volunteer work site.

Further information: www.sierraclub.org

USA ~ YELLOWSTONE NATIONAL PARK:
DANCES WITH ENDANGERED WOLVES
& GRIZZLY BEARS

BY ANDREW DEAN NYSTROM

JOHN ELK III | LPI

PHOTOLIBRARY

E ver dreamed of spending a summer with more free-roaming wildlife – bears, elk, bison, wolves – than humans for neighbours? How about falling asleep to an eerie chorus of howling wolves or adding Bear Management to your résumé?

As a volunteer scientific researcher for Yellowstone's Centre for Resources, my task was to survey the microbial diversity of the park's bountiful hydrothermal features. It sounds like a technical mouthful, but the work was a perfect excuse to escape the masses at the iconic and ever-crowded park. Highlights of my ample free time included exploring seldom-seen grizzly bear habitat and sampling the soakability of off-trail hot springs.

My favourite sleeping arrangement was a historic backcountry log cabin adjacent to a pack of 19 endangered wolves. Grizzly bear claw marks gashed the front door – warning that we ought to knock before skedaddling to the outhouse in the middle of the night!

The national park service's Volunteers-In-Parks programme sponsors a range of opportunities (including in Alaska, Hawaii and Puerto Rico), lasting from a few weeks to six months and covering everything from construction and tour guiding to digital photography and fisheries management. Unfortunately, few positions include in-park lodging, but most help locate housing nearby.

For more creative types, 29 parks, both urban and rural, offer artist-in-residence stints ranging from a week up to several months in exchange for leading public programmes or the donation of a piece of artwork.

Bottom line: time-rich, money-poor folks give back in exchange for meaningful, awe-inspiring adventures in America's wildest places.

RESPONSIBLE TRAVEL CREDENTIALS

- **Yellowstone, designated the world's first national park in 1872, was named a UN World Biosphere Reserve in 1976, and was added to the World Heritage Sites in Danger list in 1995. Volunteer-aided research projects supplement under-resourced government conservation efforts while helping to protect one of the world's largest intact temperate-zone ecosystems.**

- **Volunteering is the best way to get a hands-on, behind-the-scenes education and introduction to the unique communities that border and exist within the national parks – priceless low-impact experiences that are inaccessible to tourists.**

- **Every volunteer hour provides a much-needed financial shot in the arm. With an annual operating budget of less than US$13 per acre (just under US$10 per visitor), 2.2-million-acre Yellowstone exemplifies the challenges faced by the USA's chronically underfunded national parks system.**

WHEN TO GO

Volunteer opportunities are available year-round, with the most positions open during the summer months (between May and September). Contact individual parks for exact dates and details.

GETTING THERE

The closest international airports to Yellowstone are in Salt Lake City, Utah (630km away) and Denver, Colorado (900km). There are smaller regional airstrips in all park gateway communities.

Most volunteers receive a stipend of US$7 per day. Where in-park housing is available, it's typically shared and costs are reasonable, say around US$150 per month for a bunk in a mixed-sex dorm.

Plan on bringing your own cooking and camping gear. A bicycle is a handy form of transport at many sites. Most parks provide the specialised project-specific research equipment.

International volunteers must apply for a J-1 visa (facilitated by supervisors at sponsor parks), which requires proof of personal medical insurance. Allow at least six weeks to process the paperwork. However, if you are already in the USA on a visa, you cannot apply for a J-1 visa without first returning to your home country.

THIS PAGE: Volunteering affords a more 'intimate' experience with Yellowstone's estimated 300 to 600 grizzlies.

Pacific

FIJI ~ YASAWA:
MAKE LIKE CRUSOE ON A DESERTED SOUTH PACIFIC ISLAND
BY KERRY LORIMER

NIGEL MALONE

CASEY & ASTRID WITTE MAHANEY / LPI

Kava, the mild and socially acceptable narcotic of Fiji looks – and tastes – like something that just got scooped from a puddle. If you drink enough of it, the locals promise, you get high.

There has to be an easier way, I thought, as I accepted another proffered half-coconut shell of muddy water.

But sipping the acrid soup was a small price to pay for acceptance into village life on Navatua Island in the Yasawa group, the 16 islands scattered across the Coral Sea northwest of Fiji's main island, Viti Levu.

The Admiralty chart of Fijian waters is spattered with yellow islets and benign-looking blue shallow bits that disguise rocks and reefs that happily rip the bottom out of larger vessels.

So we'd reached Navatua by sea kayak, beginning from the aquamarine shallows of the Tavewa Island's Blue Lagoon of movie fame and paddling 18km past postcard beaches, gliding over coral reefs with schools of tiny fish leaping and glittering across our bows and turtles poking their heads above the water to watch us skim by.

A dozen pairs of tawny hands helped us haul our kayaks up the beach at Navatua. In the evening, we dressed up (ie put on a sarong) and headed to the palm-thatched meeting 'hall'.

Head of the village, Chief Sione Sadrugu, presided over the *meke* (traditional party staged in our honour). Little kids sat in the sand, wide-eyed and wild-haired as their parents and rellies swayed and sang and their big brother 'warriors' made mock feints with spears. It didn't take much cajoling (I was at spear-point, after all) to join in: in a drumbeat it was villagers and paddlers, kids and a couple of dogs, all getting sweaty together.

It was hard to leave the next day (drink enough kava, you get a hangover) but our cliché awaited us: we set up camp – Crusoe-like – on a deserted South Pacific island. Vawa perfectly matches the stereotype, with pellucid waters lapping white strips of sand overhung by palm trees.

After a week on Fiji time, I lay on the sand under a sliver of moon, pleasantly salty and sun-stung, and listened to the karaoke of wavelets and scurrying hermit crabs – with occasional percussion intervention from falling coconuts. It seemed a long way from the nightclubs of Nadi.

RESPONSIBLE TRAVEL CREDENTIALS

- Paddling a kayak and sleeping in tents makes negligible environmental impact compared with, say, staying in the beach resorts of the main island.

- In many resorts, the traditional *meke* has been transformed for tourist tastes (or lack thereof). In Navatua, it's the real deal – a genuine expression of traditional hospitality.

- Southern Sea Ventures pays camping fees to the villagers and landowners, as well as sourcing supplies and services locally wherever possible. Funds are equitably distributed among the community.

- Southern Sea Ventures also sets up an education fund, managed in conjunction with the village chiefs, with donations from clients, to pay primary and secondary school fees for village kids.

WHEN TO GO

It's mild and tropical from May to November, when the trade winds blow – depending on which direction you're heading they can make paddling a challenge or a breeze!

GETTING THERE

Take a taxi from Nadi airport to the meeting point at the Waterfront Hotel in Lautoka for the first night. Next day, transfer by boat (approximately 72km) to Tavewa Island in the Yasawas.

You'll need to be reasonably fit – some previous kayaking experience is a bonus, although there will be basic instruction given. You definitely need to be able to swim!

The degree of difficulty depends on the weather, but an average paddling day is three to four hours.

A nine-day trip including six days kayaking costs A$1965, including all meals (except Lautoka), twin share. Maximum group size is 10 paddlers plus two guides.

FACING PAGE: Previous kayaking experience is an advantage when you paddle off in search of your own deserted Yasawa island.

MICRONESIA ~ NAN MADOL:
PERFECT PREHISTORIC PORT OF CALL
BY TOM HALL

TIM ROCK LPI

If Nan Madol were located a few hundred kilometres to the northwest in Hawaii, it would be big news: the tropical Machu Picchu, Stonehenge and Venice all rolled into one. After all, the Pacific isn't exactly stuffed with breathtaking ancient sites – especially not like the one that exists in harmony with the traditions and nature of its pristine island home of Pohnpei. It is precisely what it is, where it is, that makes coming here a remarkable and essential journey.

Sitting on the edge of a lush, forested tropical island and doing a good impersonation of Atlantis, Nan Madol manages to be utterly remote yet remain connected to its surroundings. Hundreds of tiny islets are home to deserted temples, homes, bathing houses and pools, which provide a ghostly window on what life was once like on the island. Built by the Saudeleurs, early rulers of the island from roughly AD 1100 to 1300, the reasons for it's desertion are unclear. It remains a wonderful mystery at one with its surrounds.

Nan Madol is fringed with mangroves rather than beaches, which over the centuries have reclaimed the crumbling ruins of this once powerful social, religious and political centre. Touring the site is a dramatic experience, cruising or kayaking down narrow channels with only exotic birds for company.

Not many people come here, and those who do get something more than a slice of history. Pohnpei offers a fascinating window on Pacific island traditions that, while they may have abandoned Nan Madol, continue to thrive in the villages around the island. For somewhere with such powerful history, Pohnpei offers a unique mix of a sustainable welcome and few visitors. It is worth the effort to get here.

RESPONSIBLE TRAVEL CREDENTIALS

- **Kayaking or touring by small boat means you're about as in harmony with nature as you can get. However, Pohnpei is a long, long flight from anywhere, so offsetting your carbon emissions is a good way to stay green on this trip.**

- **Pohnpei is a small place and has an unhurried small-island atmosphere. Spending sensibly will make sure your stay is of genuine value. Tours to Nan Madol, and other excursions on the island, are operated by locals.**

WHEN TO GO

Make sure you visit Nan Madol at high tide. This allows visitors to explore the eerie mangrove channels that hide away many of the mysteries of the ruins.

There's no bad time of year to visit Pohnpei, but many visitors prefer the drier and less humid months of December to March.

GETTING THERE

Getting to Nan Madol will involve a journey into the unknown. You'll fly from either Hawaii, the Philippines or Japan and stop at several other remote Micronesian hideaways en route. Flights into Pohnpei land on Takatik Island, linked to Kolonia, the main town, by a mile-long causeway.

There are plenty of hotels, from budget spots starting at US$50 a double to the more upmarket Village Hotel (www .thevillagehotel.com), where the best rooms cost US$110.

Once in Kolonia, day trips to Nan Madol cost around US$50, including snorkelling. Kayaks can be arranged through hotels in Kolonia and cost around US$30 per day.

FACING PAGE: The Saudeleurs inexplicably deserted the temples and other buildings of Nan Madol around 700 years ago.

PALAU ~ ROCK ISLANDS:
THE GIANT'S REMAINS
BY TIM ROCK

TIM ROCK LPI

When you're sitting in the belly of the beast, it should be easy to repress a smile. Not in Palau. My eyes scanned the Milky Way above and the twinkling of the moonlight on the warm Pacific waves. My ears were treated to the cacophony of the jungle and the lapping of waves against a fine sand beach. I couldn't help but produce a grin of sublime satisfaction. I was nestled in the Palau Rock Islands. I was worn from a day in the sun – snorkelling, kayaking and hiking through the world's most fascinating limestone maze.

Scattered across the southwestern Pacific, Palau's Rock Islands are one of nature's great creations. Part of the country's 160km-long archipelago, they have been chiselled through the centuries by wind, waves, uplifts and tiny gnawing sea creatures called chitons. The best way to visit the Rock Islands is silently; paddling an ocean kayak and gliding without a sound through the channels and passages.

Palau's major claim to fame is its amazing sheer underwater drop-offs and schooling sharks in the south that attract scuba buffs from all over the world. Rich and diverse, it has over 1200 fish species in its waters. There are 500 corals and countless invertebrates.

The islands are home to parrots and cockatoos, fruit bats and tiny owls, cave spiders and rare plants. Many creatures are endemic to the Rock Islands and even specific parts of the Rock Islands. The birds nest where man can't go, high in the jungled tops of the islands. There are over 50 marine lakes here. These isolated brackish ponds house all sorts of marine life. Many creatures have adapted to the environment. Jellyfish have lost their sting. Gobies are overgrown. Sponges sting like fire. Scientists have only studied a few of these lakes. The most famous, Jellyfish Lake, allows you to surround yourself in literally millions of domed stingless jellies.

Environmental politics have been part of the scene in Palau for decades. It was the first place in Micronesia to declare an area off limits for the benefit of its wild creatures, creating the 70 Islands Marine Preserve in the Ngemelis Islands in the late 1950s. To this day, it is a safe haven for turtles to lay eggs and mate. Even saltwater crocodiles are sometimes seen here warming in the sun.

RESPONSIBLE TRAVEL CREDENTIALS

- **Palau's President Tommy Remengesau has spearheaded a movement to ban shark fishing throughout the Indo-Pacific. He has confiscated finning boats and set fire to pyres of shark fins, vowing that no-one shall profit from the exploitation. He has encouraged other nations in the Pacific and Asia to follow suit.**

- **A coral protection and dive-site management programme has been developed. Palau has placed certain areas of the Rock Islands off-limits to tourists, put mooring buoys at its many dive sites and established a ranger programme. There is a diver licensing mechanism to fund the buoys and pay the rangers.**

- **Palau is currently working on programmes to protect estuarine saltwater crocodiles, sea turtle mating areas and the endangered dugongs that live in its waters.**

WHEN TO GO

January through April is trade wind season with little rain. Some daily showers can be found May through August but this is also when the seas are the flattest and all dive sites are accessible.

GETTING THERE

There are daily flight connections on Continental Air Micronesia between Palau and Guam. Guam is a hub and one can connect there through many airlines from Hawaii, Japan, Hong Kong and Micronesia.

Most of the accommodation is found in the Koror area and it ranges from basic to four-star. Palau also features a number of diving live-aboards that base themselves in the south near the popular dive sites.

TONGA ~ VAVA'U: SWIMMING WITH WHALES

BY KRIS MADDEN

I am perched on the back of the boat, and feelings of both excitement and trepidation are mounting in my chest. It's crunch time and I'm about to jump into these crystal clear waters and begin swimming towards an animal that is the size of a semitrailer.

I have waited for this moment for a long time, but now that it is all too real, those last nagging fears once again surface. What if the whales bump into us – even by accident? How big a turning circle does a 15m animal weighing 40 tonnes need?

As quietly as four people who are completely out of their element can, we slip into the water, led by Annah, our experienced naturalist guide, and begin slowly swimming towards a humpback whale and her baby calf lying motionless near the surface of the water. As soon as her immense shape appears, all my fears vanish, to be replaced by an overwhelming sensation of calm and awe.

The scene under the water is spell-binding. Gracefully and effortlessly, she turns towards us, and then from beneath her, a smaller version of herself peeks out to take a look.

She seems indifferent to our presence, but keeps one watchful saucer-sized eye on both us and her young son. This is most likely the first time that he has seen creatures such as us, and his curiosity gets the better of him. With the boisterous playfulness of a child that has no fear, he makes a beeline straight towards us.

As he twirls and pirouettes around us in the water, I know that conventional whale-watching has been ruined for me forever.

The islands of Vava'u in Tonga are considered a humpback-whale 'nursery' and every year between August and October several hundred humpbacks make the annual migration from Antarctica to these warm waters to breed and give birth. Tonga is one of only three countries in the world where it is possible to swim with these mighty mammals.

It is, without a doubt, one of the most awesome wildlife experiences you will ever have.

RESPONSIBLE TRAVEL CREDENTIALS

- **Whaling was banned by Tonga in 1978 when the local population of humpbacks had been hunted almost to extinction. Some conservation groups have raised concerns about whether swimming with whales is detrimental to their wellbeing, but there exists a strong pro-whaling lobby in Tonga: if the income from whale-watching were to dry up, whale hunting may again become a serious threat.**

- **The industry is tightly monitored and only permit holders can conduct swim operations under strict guidelines.**

- **Tourism is not well developed in Tonga, and the fledgling whale-watching industry provides employment and a much-needed economic boost to this developing country.**

- **A study by the International Fund for Animal Welfare (IFAW) showed that each humpback whale in Tongan waters was worth A$20,300 a year, or A$1 million in tourism dollars during its lifetime to the Tongan economy.**

- **Travelling with a responsible tour operator is essential, both for the safety of the visitor and the welfare of the whales themselves. Whaleswim Adventures makes a contribution from the cost of each trip to whale research and conservation, and includes a strong education and conservation component in the tours.**

WHEN TO GO

Humpback whales can be seen in Tonga between August and October before they begin their migration southward back to Antarctica.

GETTING THERE

Several international airlines service Nuku'alofa, Tonga's capital. From there, Tonga's domestic carrier, Peau Vava'u, operates flights to the Vava'u island group.

There are several whale-watching operators running day trips or extended stays from the port town of Neiafu. Whaleswim Adventures operates several tours, including nine-day trips with seven days whale swimming. Accommodation is on shore in traditional *fales* (houses), from where you're picked up for daily boat excursions. The trip costs from A$3795 per person twin share, including most meals.

Maximum group size is 10 to 12 and only four people, plus one guide, are permitted in the water with the whales at any one time.

You'll need to be reasonably fit and confident swimming or snorkelling in open water.

FACING PAGE: The warm waters of Tonga are a humpback whale nursery and – with careful guidance – you can share some mutual curiosity with these leviathans.

Further information: www.tongaholiday.com | www.whaleswim.com

USA ~ HAWAII:
PARADISE FOR FREE, ALMOST
BY SAM BENSON

HOLGER LEUE LPI

Peak season is December to April, though winter can bring stormy weather and rough ocean conditions. The stiflingly hot summer months are also popular. Visiting in the in-between shoulder seasons is easier, cheaper and more serene.

GETTING THERE

Most international and domestic flights land at Honolulu International Airport, from where you can catch frequent inter-island flights (make reservations online a month in advance to grab the best fares, from US$75 each way).

Bus routes cover the island of O'ahu, with spotty local service on Maui, Kaua'i and the Big Island of Hawai'i.

Like other island destinations, a trip to Hawaii is a dream come true for most people. At least, that is, until their package tour lands in the crowded concrete jungle of Waikiki, where heat radiates off the smelly asphalt, unlovely beaches are crowded to capacity, and motel-sized resort rooms a mile from the beach still cost US$250 per night.

To find that true tropical idyll, you've got to escape Hawaii's manufactured 'condovilles' and go *au naturel*. Start by putting up your tent and living off the land. While luxury ocean-view resort rooms give no more than a glimpse of the Pacific, Hawaii's campgrounds put you on a clifftop above the surf or even right on the sand itself.

Then grab guava and papayas off a nearby tree for breakfast, or stop by the local farmers' market for fresh fare, such as seafood right off the boat. You can walk on any beach you please, no matter how pricey the resort it fronts, as all public coastal access in Hawaii is free, as guaranteed by law. Hotel guests get no special privileges.

Venture into Hawaii's phenomenal natural parks and preserves, too. Entry passes cost a fraction of the daily 'resort fee' charged at major hotels. Instead of artificial swimming pools and indoor workout rooms, you'll get volcanic peaks, tumbling waterfalls, pristine snorkelling spots, navigable rivers and bamboo-jungle hikes to explore.

With a spicy sense of adventure and a willingness to get back to basics by living more elementally, you'll find the Hawaii of your dreams – and it practically won't cost a thing.

RESPONSIBLE TRAVEL CREDENTIALS

- **High-rise hotels, beachfront resorts and golf courses have a detrimental impact on Hawaii's fragile ecosystem. By avoiding these places, you'll help protect the islands' unique natural resources, including freshwater streams, wildlife habitats and beaches.**

- **Outside the resort complexes, you'll have a greater chance of interacting with locals and experiencing genuine Hawaiian culture as opposed to prepackaged luaus.**

- **If you plan an outdoors-oriented vacation in Hawaii, what you spend goes directly into local communities and national, state and county parks systems instead of multinational corporations that don't invest in the islands.**

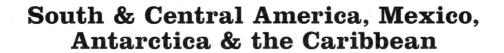

South & Central America, Mexico, Antarctica & the Caribbean

ANTARCTICA ~ ANTARCTIC PENINSULA: CRUISING IN THE WHITE WILDERNESS
BY KERRY LORIMER

KERRY LORIMER

KERRY LORIMER

A soft fog hung over the bay, amplifying and isolating the pops and groans of the glaciers as they calved icebergs into water that had the smoothness and sheen of mercury.

Standing alone on the bow of the ship, I was startled by a sound like a bursting car tyre. I leaned over the cap-rail and looked straight into the blowhole of a humpback whale.

Minutes later we were in the inflatable Zodiac boats, nudging through the brash ice as whales surfaced all around us. A huge male breached, heaving his 40-tonne bulk clear of the water and crashing down with a thunderous splash. For the next hour he 'performed' for us: breaching, tail slapping and occasionally approaching so close to the Zodiacs we could smell his fishy breath.

Such wondrous wildlife interactions are a daily – even hourly – occurrence in Antarctica. Hundreds of thousands of penguins stretch like 3-D wallpaper as far as you can see. If you sit at the edge of a rookery, you'll soon find yourself surrounded: the birds haven't read the rules on minimum-approach distances. Albatrosses wheel effortlessly about the ship on the passage through the Southern Ocean; elephant seals, lying in scrofulous heaps like monstrous mouldy cigars, belch and fart with casual disinterest.

Antarctica is, arguably, the most beautiful place on earth – a pristine wilderness where ice takes on every rainbow hue, where the wildlife is astonishingly prolific and without fear of man, and where you are utterly at the mercy of the elements. It's nature at her most raw and powerful. I was awed and humbled by my first visit – and I've looked at the world differently ever since.

RESPONSIBLE TRAVEL CREDENTIALS

- **There are now more than 30 cruise-ship operators working in Antarctica, with vessels ranging from 400-passenger ocean liners to 50- or 100-passenger ice-strengthened 'expedition-style' ships, most of which were built for the Russian scientific programme before the USSR collapsed. All are required to abide by the strictest minimum-environmental-impact guidelines, as stipulated by the Independent Association of Antarctic Tour Operators (IAATO) and in accordance with the Protocol on Environmental Protection to the Antarctic Treaty (1991).**

- **One of the larger operators Peregrine claims to lead the way in environmental responsibility. Among other measures, all its Zodiacs run four-stroke outboards (cleaner than two-stroke), and it maintains a high guide-to-client ratio and a comprehensive client educational programme. The company also supports a range of scientific projects and has raised over A$300,000 for albatross conservation.**

WHEN TO GO

Voyages depart between November and March.

GETTING THERE

The Antarctic Peninsula is the most popular and accessible part of Antarctica – it's two days' sailing from Ushuaia, at the southern tip of South America, across the infamous Drake Passage, and has the highest concentration of wildlife on the continent. There are also voyages from Tasmania, New Zealand and South Africa, travelling to the Ross Sea and remote emperor penguin rookeries.

Travelling with an 'expedition-style' operator will ensure maximum time ashore or Zodiac cruising – usually averaging two to three excursions daily. Tips for selecting an operator: make sure there are enough Zodiacs to get all passengers on the water at once (avoiding 'shuttles'); choose a fast ship (the less time you spend 'at sea' the more time you have in Antarctica); a sophisticated stabilisation system will help stave off seasickness.

Peninsula voyages follow similar routings for most operators. For example, Peregrine offers trips from 10 to 19 nights, visiting the Antarctic Peninsula as well as South Georgia and the Falkland Islands. Its prices start at around A$8500 per person, twin share, including all taxes, meals and excursions.

THIS PAGE: When you find a solitary moment to contemplate your place in the natural scheme of things, the sense of vastness and humility you get in Antarctica is overwhelming.

FACING PAGE: The Antarctic Peninsula is the 'extension' of the Andes – mountains rise up to 300m directly out of the ocean. On a clear day, a barbecue on the aft deck gives the best float-by view.

Further information: www.iaato.org | www.peregrineadventures.com

Culture Shock vs Cultural Connection

After that initial attack of culture shock – that in-your-face, unsettling assault on the senses of a new and foreign culture – wears off, you'll inevitably find that many of your most fun, meaningful and memorable travel experiences are the times you make a personal connection with someone from a world wholly different to your own.

It may be as simple as sharing a joke or a meal, it may be travelling the same road or working on a project towards a common goal. The essence of these experiences is sharing, an equitable exchange – and mutual enjoyment!

Open-mindedness, understanding and respect go a long way to easing you out of culture shock and into cultural acceptance. It's sometimes easy to judge someone else's culture by your own assumptions and social mores, but try dropping your expectations and accepting that others' customs are not wrong, just different.

A few basic tips for making mutually enjoyable cultural connections:

- Go with the flow – other cultures have very different concepts of time, personal space and socially acceptable behaviour, among other things. You'll find it a lot less stressful – and a lot more enlightening – if you just chill out. You might even reassess your own ideas.

- Remember you're a guest in someone else's home/village/community – the basic rule of 'do unto others' applies overseas as it does in your own backyard. Respect people's privacy and private property – ask permission if you want to enter or interrupt an activity, or to take a photo. And abide by the laws of the country.

- Dress appropriately – looking at the locals is a good way to gauge what to wear. In some countries – particularly Muslim ones, and in the Indian Subcontinent – it is offensive to flash your flesh, particularly if you're a woman. If you do, you'll just be confirming suspect ideas about Western women, as well as attracting unwanted attention. If you dress and behave appropriately, you're far less likely to be sexually harassed and far more likely to be treated with respect. In Latin America, even the poorest people strive to look neat and clean, so grubby or torn clothing is considered disrespectful. And leave the bling at home – flashy jewellery not only

makes you a target for thieves, it's a tactless reminder of the disparity between your wealth and the locals' lack.

- Be respectful in places of worship such as churches, mosques or temples. This means dressing respectfully – long trousers for men and long skirts or trousers for women. You may be required to remove your hat at some temples, while at mosques you should cover your head (women are generally not allowed into the main prayer hall). At both temples and mosques, remove your shoes. At Hindu temples, you will sometimes have to remove leather objects such as belts before entering.

- Try to be conservative with resources such as water, food and energy – you may be depriving local people or making a negative impact on their environs.

- Buying locally made crafts and curios means your money goes directly to the community. But be sure the vendor is not being pressured into selling something he/she doesn't really want to sell, either because of economic desperation or through traditional politeness.

- Enjoy the ancient art of bargaining: part pas de deux, part drama, part chess-game, bargaining is a skill and an art form. It's as much about the social interaction as the final outcome. It's about fair trade, and reaching a balance that suits both participants. Have fun with it and keep things in perspective – does haggling over that last dollar really make a difference to you, compared to the vendor? (Bargaining is not a part of all cultures, so make sure you know where and when it's appropriate to haggle and when you might cause offence.)

- In many countries it is just not on for couples to show any emotion towards each other in public – if you can't keep your hands, lips and tongues off each other then you'll have to stay in your room until you can bear to walk down the street together in compatible isolation.

Clearly, most of this is common sense: meeting and getting on with people overseas follows the same rules as back home, just with a few culturally specific quirks. Nevertheless, it's constantly astounding how many travellers manage to leave their manners at home.

'Cultural sensitivity' is simply a matter of respect: take your behavioural cues from the locals and, if in doubt, try to see things from the locals' point of view, or ask yourself how you'd like a visitor to behave in your home town.

Making friends on your travels won't always be simple: in some cases you'll find local people may be aloof or even suspicious of you. Given the antics of many less socially aware travellers, you could hardly blame them.

And there are, of course, weirdos and crooks in every society. The trick is to avoid generalisations: just because a taxi driver ripped you off in Lima doesn't mean all Peruvian taxi drivers are thieves!

When you do make that cross-cultural connection – even though initially you may have thought you had nothing in common – you realise that people are essentially the same all over the world. We all have the same needs and desires, aspirations and affections – albeit with different culturally specific nuances. Both parties sharing that realisation – and revelling in it – is the holy grail of travelling.

BAHAMAS ~ EXUMA:
SAILING IN AN ISLAND HEAVEN

BY JILL KIRBY

Exuma in the Bahamas has two claims to fame. Two James Bond movies, *Thunderball* and *Never Say Never Again*, were shot around Staniel Cay in the Exuma Cays Land and Sea Park. This 280-sq-km island and ocean preserve was also the first 'marine replenishment nursery' in the world, initiated in 1958. It has successfully protected marine species from overfishing.

Virtually off the tourism radar, it is also a stunning natural playground for sailors. Hire a small sailboat to explore the park's uninhabited and pristine white-sand isles and camp under the stars. Novice and experienced yachties revel in sailing glorious turquoise seas, while divers and snorkellers can immerse themselves in a myriad of marine life.

Bahamian seas have been described as the most beautiful on earth. Buy supplies and hire a sailboat (beginners welcome) and camping gear in Great Exuma, the head of Exuma's necklace of 365 isles, and head off for a few weeks of adventure.

The Exuma Cays Land and Sea Park runs 35km south from Wax Cay Cut to Conch Cut and Fowl Cay, encompassing 10 islands and numerous smaller cays. Run by the Bahamas National Trust, all creatures within the park, whether feathered, scaled or furry, have been protected since the mid-1980s.

On land you can follow nature trails and explore the ruins of 18th-century Loyalist settlements, caves, and bird and wildlife reserves. The islands are home to endangered Bahamian iguanas and hutias, reminiscent of large guinea pigs, as well as elegant white-tailed tropic birds. Dolphins and large rays fly through the park seas, alongside an abundance of neon-coloured fish, coral reefs, blue holes and ancient shipwrecks.

RESPONSIBLE TRAVEL CREDENTIALS

- **Park visitors must adhere to a list of strict regulations. These prohibit fishing, hunting and removing objects from the reserve.**

- **The marine reserve is now recognised as an economic benefit; a major tourism attraction that replenishes stocks of seafood. Populations of conch, an endangered species and staple Bahamian protein, are 31 times higher inside than outside the park. Tagged lobsters have been found repopulating areas around Cat Island (112km away) and around 74% of dangerously overfished grouper in the northern Exuma region originates from the park.**

- **By supporting tourism that does not require infrastructure, you can help locals fight against development within the park, which is an ongoing threat.**

- **The dollars you spend on hiring boats and buying supplies will go straight into local pockets and the local economy – income levels are generally low in the region.**

- **Many Bahamian island tourism developments are decimating bird, wildlife and marine habitats. By visiting the park you support the creation of similar marine and land reserves across the Bahamas and the national work of the self-funded NGO Bahamas National Trust (www.bahamasnationaltrust.com).**

WHEN TO GO

May to October may see some rain, but rates are cheaper than in the winter 'peak' times of mid-December to mid-April. Lying on the edge of the Caribbean's hurricane belt, the Bahamian hurricane season is from June to November.

GETTING THERE

Fly direct from the USA or take a ferry or plane from New Providence to Great Exuma. In George Town hire a sailboat (US$700 per week) from Starfish, a local company that also rents sea kayaks.

BOLIVIA ~ MADIDI NATIONAL PARK: RUSTIC ROOMS IN REMOTE ENCLAVE

BY DAVID ATKINSON

In February 2005 a team of researchers from the Wildlife Conservation Society discovered a new species of titi monkey in the Madidi National Park, a remote enclave of Bolivia described by NGO Conservation International as the most biologically diverse protected area on the planet. The discovery put Madidi firmly on the tourist map, leading to rapid moves to develop several so-called 'ecolodges' strung out along the Rivers Beni and Tuichi in Bolivian Amazonia.

The original and most genuinely sustainable lodge, however, remains Chalalan, which celebrates its 10th anniversary in 2005 as Bolivia's most successful ever responsible-tourism project.

'We were worried about the exodus of people from the rainforest community. By 1985, over 50% of families had left in search of work, so we sought a project to manage tourism to benefit the community,' says Guido Mamami, a village Elder turned general manager of Chalalan, as we motor upriver in a souped-up canoe.

We pull up by the riverbank from where a gentle walk along a nature trail brings us to the Chalalan lodge, a clutch of wood and palm-built cabins dipping their stilted toes into the warm waters of Lake Chalalan.

The cabins are simple and rustic, some with en suite bathrooms and solar-powered showers. All rooms come with mosquito nets and fresh towels, while meals, including a traditional supper of catfish cooked in leaves, are served in a central dining hall.

Nature hikes are the main activity with 14 well-marked nature trails encircling the lodge. Most walks set out at first light and return for a shower, relaxed lunch and a lazy afternoon swinging in the hammocks.

It's a simple silver plaque on a tree stump in the grounds, however, that best sums up the spirit of Chalalan. It reads: 'Living in harmony with nature…a dream made reality.'

JAMES LYON LIPI

RESPONSIBLE TRAVEL CREDENTIALS

- Madidi commands 11% of the world's species of flora and fauna, including 10,000 tree and 1100 animal species. Hunting and logging had taken their toll on the region, but since both Madidi was declared a protected area and the Chalalan lodge developed in 1995, flora and fauna have returned.

- Chalalan now attracts 1000 tourists annually and turns over a healthy US$25,000 profit, paying a share to the 74 families from the jungle pueblo of San José de Uchupiamonas working at the lodge. Profits are also used to build community health and education facilities.

- After several years of assistance from international NGOs, Chalalan has been handed back to the indigenous Quechua-Tacana community to be managed entirely by local people.

WHEN TO GO

Flights to Rurrenabaque are often cancelled during rainy season (December to March); Chalalan books up with tour groups July to September, so plan ahead.

GETTING THERE

America Tours in La Paz offers a three-night jungle package for US$279 per person, twin share, with two nights in Chalalan on a full-board basis.

There's an additional US$10 entrance fee to Madidi National Park payable locally, and return flights from La Paz to Rurrenabaque with Amazonas from US$110.

Further information: www.chalalan.com in Spanish | www.america-ecotours.com

BRAZIL ~ RÍO NEGRO:
PROTECTING THE PANTANAL
BY KERRY LORIMER

MELINDA NYE | EARTHWATCH

N ow your Brazilian giant otter isn't your average furry fish eater. At about 2m in length and weighing up to 30kg, he's a fairly formidable predator. His tail has a 'keel' and his mouth is set like a shark's. While he's not too fast on land, he's perfectly adapted to the rivers of the Amazon and Brazil's Pantanal – the world's largest freshwater wetland. Or at least he was until river systems became polluted, beef prices headed south and fashionistas decreed otter fur the best thing in coats.

Where once the Pantanal's remoteness in southwestern Brazil ensured its relative sanctity, more intensive cattle ranching, mining, dam building – and even tourism – are now impacting on its fragile ecosystem.

Earthwatch has established a Conservation Research Initiative (CRI) consisting of nine separate, but integrated, volunteer-supported research programmes, covering aquatic ecology and amphibians to bats, birds, peccaries and pigs – and, of course, otters. The data collected by volunteers will help the development of a network of private and publicly owned protected areas and corridors linking critical habitat areas in the Pantanal and the associated Cerrado. Given the Pantanal is the size of Iowa (210,000 sq km), it's an ambitious vision, and one that must work in concert with local community needs.

Besides the otters, there are around 30 million caimans lurking in the Pantanal, which embraces a diverse range of habitats and the greatest concentration of wildlife in South America. There are anacondas the thickness of a thigh, maned wolves, tapirs, the world's largest jaguars, and the semi-aquatic, oversized rodents, the capybaras. All up, there are around 100 species of mammals, 650 types of birds and 260 species of fish, including one that eats fruit…as it swims through the treetops in the seasonal floods.

Volunteers sign up for one of the nine expeditions, but will frequently work across a variety of field assignments, which gives a better understanding of the scope of the CRI. A focus of the Otter Ecology and Conservation project is studying the impact of tourism. Being handsome and playful, otters have great tourism potential; however, they are sensitive to human disturbance. Volunteers' observations of nesting and social behaviour will help determine the requirements for the otters' health, with the results presented to policy-makers and the public.

This project is conservation overlaid with the irrepressible carnival attitude of Brazilians. While your days may be filled with otter scat (fascinating as it is), your evenings are likely to revolve around sipping *caipirinhas* with the local cowboys and dancing the bossanova into the wee hours.

RESPONSIBLE TRAVEL CREDENTIALS

- **The CRI was established in partnership with Conservation International (CI) Brazil. It's an ambitious attempt to study a series of interconnected issues and link them together in an overall conservation strategy for a very large ecosystem. It has the potential to be a model for successfully balancing large-scale biodiversity conservation with maintaining the livelihoods of local people.**

- **An aim of the CRI is to establish partnerships, outreach and environmental education programmes with local communities. The issues identified by local partners feed the research agenda, with the aim being to find supplementary or alternative income sources for communities. One possibility is controlled responsible tourism: the otter project seeks to set some guidelines.**

- **Earthwatch is a not-for-profit organisation that supports conservation projects by enabling paying volunteers to work alongside scientists in the field.**

WHEN TO GO

Expeditions run virtually year-round. Be prepared for tropical conditions: pack the bug spray.

GETTING THERE

The CRI, including the Otter Ecology and Conservation project and eight other expeditions, is situated in the Brazilian state of Mato Grosso do Sul on the Río Negro in the southern Pantanal.

The rendezvous point for the expedition is Campo Grande, which can be accessed by a two-hour flight from São Paulo.

Projects cost from US$1895 per person for seven days or from US$2495 for 12 days, including all meals, training and a financial contribution to the project. No previous experience is necessary.

Accommodation is generally in comfortable farmhouses and/or research stations on a twin-share basis.

THIS PAGE: Giant otters grow to 2m in length.

FACING PAGE: Poling a dugout canoe is the best way to get around on the shallow, reed-thick waters of the Pantanal. It's also the ideal moving platform for viewing the 650 species of bird that inhabit the world's largest wetland.

Further information: www.earthwatch.org

CHILE ~ RÍO FUTALEUFÚ: WHITE-WATER WILDERNESS

BY KERRY LORIMER

Doodle a finger across a map of Chilean Patagonia and you'll find there are few roads to trace, and fewer towns to point to. The most striking feature after the crazy-paving coastline of shattered islets is the rivers: flowing from the hanging-glacier heights of the Andes, they are the key to accessing some of the most remote and spectacular wilderness on the planet.

The Río Futaleufú isn't so much a key as a battering ram: it forces its way between granite peaks and hammers at rock walls with a fury that produces some of the world's best white water for rafting. Riding the Fu is not for the faint-hearted or the unfit. Class III/IV and optional Class V rapids will have you paddling for your life – and if (or when) you get catapulted from your raft into the foaming maw of 'Terminator' or 'Tiburon' (meaning 'shark'), you better be able to swim. Hard.

If the stuffing isn't scared out of you on the 'introductory' rapids and your rafting guide deems you fit enough (and able to follow orders with the unquestioning response of a storm trooper) you get a shot at the river's most technical rapids, the Class V Infierno Canyon. Here the river is pinched between rock walls to a 30m-wide frothing torrent that seethes over three plummeting drops in a row. When the guide yells 'High side!' you jump – and pray.

If you are stuffing-less (or just stuffed) by this stage, you get to walk around the rapids: two hours through virgin rainforest. Then, after a momentary gentle float, the Fu reaches full ferocity: 'Zeta' and the 'Throne Room' command porterages, but are followed by a cruiser romp through the 'Wild Mile' rapids.

Rafting the Fu involves two nights under canvas (complete with improvised sauna) on a riverside beach overlooked by three nuns: the base of the granite spires of Tres Monjas is the destination focus for a lay-day hike.

A day later, the Fu's wave-train rapids are a series of fun – and terrifying – tests of faith in the float-ability of your boat and the paddling ability of your guide and fellow crew. Over three days, the river flows through stunning wilderness – valleys, canyons and rainforest – which is otherwise completely inaccessible. The only way to see it is to face the fury of the Fu.

RESPONSIBLE TRAVEL CREDENTIALS

- **Rafting is one of the most minimum-impact modes of transport. The guides also follow a minimum-impact policy at the camp site.**

- **US$10 of your trip cost goes to local conservation group Futafriends, which is campaigning to prevent the construction of a series of proposed dams on the river. As an alternative future, Futafriends supports Chilean groups working to develop responsible tourism, small-scale agriculture and increased opportunities for the local community.**

- **Your participation and vocal opposition to the dam construction helps raise the profile of the area as an adventure travel destination, which makes it more difficult from a PR perspective for the energy company to progress its plans.**

- **Local people are now seeing the value of tourism (which provides direct cash benefits) over hydro schemes (which benefit distant shareholders) and are becoming more forcefully opposed to the dams.**

WHEN TO GO

Trips run between December and March.

GETTING THERE

Mountain Travel Sobek offers a nine-day Río Futaleufú adventure, which includes three days white-water rafting, as well as mountain-bike riding, hiking, sea kayaking, and optional horse-riding and canyoneering.

It departs from Santiago (Chile) and includes six nights in lodge accommodation and two nights deluxe camping, with all meals included. It costs from US$2590 per person, plus US$385 for internal flights.

CHILE ~ TORRES DEL PAINE NATIONAL PARK: PERFECT HORSE-RIDING COUNTRY

BY GISELLE RADULOVIC

RICHARD I'ANSON | LPI

BRENT WINEBRENNER/LPI

W e're at the end of the world at the edge of the southern ice fields, our horses basking in the late afternoon sun, the wine chilling in the shallows of the shimmering glacial Laguna Azul. In the adjacent *quincho* (country cabin used for barbecues) the fireplace is being prepared for a traditional *asado* (lamb on the spit) and the long table inside is set for the evening's festivities.

Southern Patagonia: in terms of population density, we're in one of the remotest inhabited regions in the world. But it's New Year's Eve and for our group of 12 the celebrations are just about to start.

The backdrop to our camp site is three spectacular *torres* (towers of granite), their tops lightly dusted with snow. Reaching nearly 3000m among the peaks of the Cordillera del Paine mountain range they are the centrepieces of Torres del Paine National Park in Chilean Patagonia, in the southernmost region of South America. Flanked by Argentina to the east and an intricate network of subantarctic fjords to the west, the park is a wonderland of ancient southern beech forest, glaciers, granite mountains, fast-running rivers, expansive pampas and ample wildlife.

Uninterrupted by fences, roads or urban development, it's perfect horse-riding country. And so, adopting the traditional transport of the local community, we had mounted our sturdy *criollo* (a horse descended from the Spanish horses imported by the conquistadores in the 16th century) just over a week ago and began crisscrossing the park via a well-disguised network of mountain trails, river crossings, valley descents and exhilarating canters across the pampas.

From our initial hesitant trot around the turquoise shores of Laguna Verde, we ventured into thick virgin forests, ascended steep trails for mesmerising views of the pampas and lakes, picked our way across the hills of the Sierra Contreras and got close enough to see the deep blue cracks of a southern ice-fields glacier.

Along the way we encountered families of elegant guanaco and large groups of ostrich-like rhea, while high above us Andean condors tracked our progress, black specks in a bright blue sky.

And now it's New Year's Eve and there are no fireworks, no giant ticking clock and no gatecrashers to our party. How very civilised, I think, warming my toes by the fire, my body pleasantly tired after a long day in the saddle.

RESPONSIBLE TRAVEL CREDENTIALS

- **Horse-riding and wilderness camping is a low-impact way of exploring the area, rather than following the few well-trodden hiking trails. Instead of vehicles, pack-horses are used to move luggage and supplies between camp sites.**

- **Local *baqueanos* (Chilean gauchos) are employed to ride with the groups and take care of the horses, providing a direct link with the community. The tack used for the horses is Chilean and comprises metal-framed saddles with leather, felt and sheepskin layers.**

- **Chileans make up three-quarters of BlueGreen Adventures' workforce. Food and supplies are purchased locally from Puerto Natales. BlueGreen Adventures also offers an itinerary that utilises locally owned accommodation including a working estancia (ranch) within Torres del Paine National Park.**

WHEN TO GO

Trips operate during the summer months from November to March. However, the weather can be very unpredictable and it's possible to experience four seasons in a few hours! Average daily temperatures vary but in summer expect 10°C to 20°C with the occasional hot day of 25°C. Temperatures can drop to zero at night and high winds are common.

GETTING THERE

To get to Patagonia from Chile's capital, Santiago, take a domestic flight to Punta Arenas (three to four hours). BlueGreen Adventures will meet you on arrival.

You will need to have intermediate to advanced riding experience and be able to control a horse on open ground at a canter. Some of the riding days are long so stamina and a can-do attitude are a must!

Minimum group size is two and the maximum 12, plus a guide and *baqueanos* to care for the horses.

A 12-day trip with eight days of riding starts at US$2550 per person including all meals (except in Punta Arenas and Puerto Natales on the final day).

FACING PAGE: The Torres del Paine soar to 3km above the pampas, dwarfing riders and their horses.

CUBA ~ HAVANA:
SIX DEGREES EXPERIENCE
BY KERRY LORIMER

You could go to Cuba, lie on the groomed beaches and take the government-sanctioned salsa lessons in the hermetically-sealed resorts of Varadero and never experience the Six Degrees of Cuba.

In Cuba, everyone knows somebody who has a friend who has a cousin who can help you out: utilising the network to get around the country will get you into the rhythm of Cuba better than any Varadero dance class.

The best way to join this game is to find a *casa particular* – the Cuban version of a home-stay – that you really like. And to kick-start the Six Degrees experience you should find this by referral: ask a friend – they're bound to have a friend who knows someone who stayed somewhere really good.

Casas vary enormously in quality in a given price range – you might find yourself in a high-ceilinged salon with views of the *malecón* (waterfront promenade) or a poky apartment – so the initial referral is vital. Once you've found a nice place and a friendly owner (it's not hard) you've got the starting link of a chain that, when followed, can take you all over the island and introduce you to families – and their friends – from all walks of Cuban life.

Your *casa* owner in Havana will know someone in Trinidad who has a lovely home and can phone ahead to book a room for you. Senora Trinidad will have a sister-in-law in Santiago who not only takes in lodgers but has a son who teaches salsa.

Guidebooks and those travelling on the cheap complain that the *casa* owners get a kickback of around US$5 for a referral, and this is undoubtedly common (but not universal) practice. So what? If it means that there's a friendly face waiting for you at the bus stop with a car or a cousin to carry your gear and you don't have to run the gauntlet of the *jineteros* (street hustlers) it's a bargain.

More than that, *you're* coming recommended, which gives you an entrée to family life and the Cuban neighbour network that glues the community together and keeps the country running. You want fish for dinner? Well, the old man next door just hauled in a monster and there's plenty for everyone. Cousin Juan plays guitar – mix in some rum and you've got yourselves a fiesta. (You may or may not end up footing the bill, but it's way more fun than getting boozed in the Varadero bars.)

It's not impossible to just go with the flow and allow yourself to be passed – parcel-like – around the country. Of course, it won't always be sun and salsa – the usual travel scams and precautions still apply, especially in Havana – but when the wheels fall off (probably literally) – those old cars don't run forever) you can usually find somebody with a spanner.

Just remember when you get back home to tell a friend – they're sure to have a cousin who has a sister who wants to go to Cuba.

RESPONSIBLE TRAVEL CREDENTIALS

- **Voracious hotel development along the north coast (catering virtually exclusively to foreigners) continues to severely impact prime habitat for many unique birds and reptiles. In contrast, *casa particulares* are often in Heritage-listed homes, where your cash may help with the upkeep.**

- **Cubans are banned from entering tourist resort hotels unless they work there, and are generally restricted from interacting with foreigners. Behind the 'closed doors' of the *casa*, you start to get the inside take on all things Cuban, and might correct a few misconceptions about the world beyond the island.**

- **Your *casa*-spent dollars circumvent the pockets of Castro and his cronies – and their international partners – who own and operate almost all Cuba's hotels, effectively excluding the general population from the US-dollar economy (although *casa* owners still pay heavy taxes).**

WHEN TO GO
December to March has the least rain and humidity. September to November is hurricane season.

GETTING THERE
There are *casa particulares* virtually everywhere in Cuba – some you can book before you leave home (see guidebooks for listings). Alternatively, you could book a hotel for your first night in Cuba and phone ahead for further nights. Prices vary, with cities being more expensive. Expect to pay between US$15 and US$40 per night, per room – usually there's no discount for singles. It's advisable to stick to licensed premises, identifiable by a sticker on the front door.

Casa owners will normally provide meals for an additional charge – usually less than government restaurants and with much better food. You may be able to make special requests.

FACING PAGE: Looking for an entrée into Cuban community? Join a game of dominos – favourite pastime of Cubans in a hot climate.

Further information: good sources for *casa particulares* recommendations are fellow travellers, guidebooks and the Lonely Planet Thorn Tree – http://thorntree.lonelyplanet.com

ECUADOR ~ GALÁPAGOS ISLANDS: EXPLORING NATURAL WONDERS

BY DON GEORGE

The Galápagos Epiphany struck me after the others in my walking tour had moved on and I was a temporary castaway on the island of Genovesa: black-and-white Nazca boobies squabbled in front of me, red-pouched frigate birds wheeled over me, a juvenile red-footed booby fluttered uncertainly onto a branch at my back and bellowing sea lions snout-fenced on my right – all gloriously indifferent to my presence. I looked out onto glittering Darwin Bay and felt like old Charles himself.

My 16-year-old daughter's GE occurred when she was adopted by a duo of acrobatic sea lions off a volcanic clump of an island called Champion. For 20 minutes they sleeked, slid and somersaulted over, around and alongside her, urging her to follow them, until they bade farewell with whiskery waves. When she slipped breathless onto our boat, Jenny said that for a few moments she felt like she really was a sea lion.

The GE hit my 12-year-old son when we turned a corner on Espanola to discover a blue-footed female booby right in the middle of the path – and right in the midst of lifting herself to reveal a bright white egg. At that moment, the shell cracked and a new, wet chick appeared. Jeremy watched, stunned, as it struggled into the world and its mother plopped protectively over it: evolution in action.

And the GE touched my wife one morning as she watched Sally Lightfoot crabs, land and marine iguanas, sea lions, boobies and gulls – all these different species – peacefully sharing the same small patch of island. 'Maybe someday humans will learn to get along so well,' she sighed as tears pooled in her eyes.

The Galápagos are a chain of more than 120 volcanic islands and islets located 970km off the coast of Ecuador. Ancient mariners called them the Enchanted Islands because they seemed to shift location, but my family calls them the Enchanted Islands because they delivered the most magical and fulfilling vacation we have ever had.

The Galápagos present a world where man is not feared as a predator but either ignored or simply studied as a curious new species. The extraordinary reality of this alternate universe doesn't hit until you are there and a swallow-tailed gull simply cocks an inquisitive eye at you, or a sea lion surfs a wave right behind you, or a marine iguana stays statuesquely still as you shuffle by. As a visitor to the Galápagos, you see how wildlife has adapted to a human-less environment and you are given the opportunity to interact with these fearless species in a singular way. And of course, you also get to pay homage to the site of the original GE: Darwin's revolutionary theory of natural selection, which took seed here in 1835 with the humble observation of a finch's beak – and which went on to fundamentally influence the course of Western thought.

Our Galápagos odyssey gave my family a memory that will bind us for the rest of our days – and it gave me the hope that perhaps like the islands' first wind-blown and wave-borne inhabitants, we human visitors are unwitting accomplices in a greater evolution: bringing back seeds of peace and wonder to plant in the hard rock of our larger world.

RESPONSIBLE TRAVEL CREDENTIALS

- Every tour must be accompanied by national park–certified naturalists who both provide information and ensure stringent wildlife protection regulations are adhered to.

- Ninety per cent of the entry fee every visitor pays (US$100) is retained by the Galápagos, with 40% going to the national park, 40% to local authorities and the remainder to other local interests.

WHEN TO GO

December to April tends to be warmer and wetter and the sea is generally calmer; from June to November a fine mist frequently falls and the vegetation is lusher. Either season is spectacularly rewarding.

GETTING THERE

To reach the Galápagos, fly to Quito or Guayaquil in Ecuador and connect to Baltra, the islands' principal airport and cruise embarkation point.

Galápagos cruise options run the gamut from bare-bones operations to sleek, high-end ships. My family travelled on a 10-day trip (which means six days actually cruising the islands) with Lindblad Expeditions, which sponsors a number of Galápagos-based programmes dedicated to conservation and education. The 10-day cruise costs from US$3650.

FACING PAGE: A blue-footed booby appears more indignant than afraid of humans.

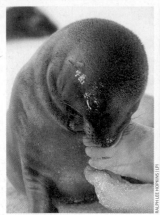

The Galápagos Under Threat

BY KERRY LORIMER

The Galápagos were declared the world's first Natural World Heritage site in 1978 and a Unesco Biosphere Reserve in 1984 and have one of the longest-running successful models of 'responsible tourism'. Even so, the islands are still under threat.

Responsible tourism has been an economic boom for the islands and is the mainstay for supporting the upkeep of the national park. However, tourism has increased dramatically in recent years and there is much debate as to what point to place a limit on visitor numbers. There needs to be closer monitoring of tourism impacts (particularly accidentally introduced species, pollutants, and overuse of sites and the limited water supply) and development.

The islands are also under intense pressure from the rapidly increasing resident human population: settlers from mainland Ecuador continue to arrive, despite restrictions on immigration. The majority are not qualified to work in tourism, so the alternative is fishing. Illegal fishing has had dramatic impacts, and clashes between local fishermen and national park authorities have, at times, turned violent.

While the overall plan of management for the islands has been very effective, one area that is perhaps lacking is in providing financial returns to residents. They must see some benefit – both financial and long-term – if they are to protect their natural heritage.

These issues are being addressed by government and other agencies including tour operators and NGOs. Collaboration among various agencies resulted in the Special Law for the Galápagos, although enforcement has, to date, been patchy.

The Galápagos provide one of the planet's most astounding wildlife experiences, but it's a fragile balance: as a traveller, if you can be aware of – and aim to minimise – your impact, you'll help to maintain that balance.

THIS PAGE (LEFT TO RIGHT): Playful Galápagos fur seal pup; Sally Lightfoot crab; photographing marine iguanas.

FACING PAGE: The Galápagos Islands are under increasing pressure from tourism – albeit generally well-managed 'eco-tourism'. Be mindful of minimum wildlife approach distances and your personal impact.

ECUADOR ~ KAPAWI: MEET THE ACHUAR & FEEL THE AMAZON

BY RICHARD FIELD

I had been warned about *nijiamanch*. It is the most important food/drink of the Achuar people who live in the upper Amazon rainforest bordering Ecuador and Peru. Visit an Achuar village and a bowl of *nijiamanch* will be thrust into your hands, and it is considered a great insult not to partake. It is made from pre-chewed manioc, which is spat into a vat and left to ferment – and it looks as appetising as it sounds. I even had a special visitor – a large insect doing backstroke in the gruel. The chief's wife who was handing out the drink plunged her hand into the bowl, scooped out the bug and threw it onto the dirt floor. Problem solved and smiles all around. The ladies left the room and it was now time to talk and drink!

Fortunately pretending to drink is OK; otherwise the Achuar might have significantly fewer visitors. Also I wasn't there to get drunk on fermented spit – tempting though it was – but rather to meet these incredible people who up until the early 1970s were essentially unknown to the Western world. Unlike many of the Amazon's indigenous groups, the Achuar have since been able to grow and thrive, while maintaining the bulk of their traditions (head-hunting being a notable exception). They are also part-owners of Kapawi Ecolodge and Reserve, tucked away in the Ecuadorian Amazon, close to the Peruvian border.

The lodge was built using the Achuar concept of architecture (not a single nail was used in the entire construction), and offers guests a range of activities. Walks in the forest with Achuar tribesmen reveal an intimacy and understanding that most Westerners cannot begin to comprehend. Other activities include bird-watching, canoe trips, fishing trips, multiple-day camping excursions and visits to the local village – *nijiamanch* time!

Yet what really separates Kapawi from many of the Amazon's other 'ecolodges' is the unique nature of the partnership between the Achuar and the local tour company, Canodros.

RICHARD FIELD & REBECCA FRASER

Canodros pays the Achuar a significant annual rental and a share of the profits. It is also training the Achuar with the aim of handing over the entire operation to them in 2011.

Even more important than the money is what Kapawi represents to the Achuar. In an area that is increasingly threatened by oil exploration, Kapawi demonstrates a viable alternative to drilling, and symbolises the independence and strength of the Achuar people.

RESPONSIBLE TRAVEL CREDENTIALS

- **Kapawi Ecolodge was developed in part to show indigenous communities that they do have economic options other than oil exploration, logging and cattle ranching.**

- **Guests leave Kapawi with a much greater understanding of the Achuar people as well as the Amazon. All interactions with the Achuar are authentic and on their terms. Guests are instructed on how to be respectful to the people of the community.**

- **The Achuar see direct financial benefits through their shares in the company and the rental paid to them by Canodros. Kapawi also buys products and services for the lodge in the nearby communities. The Achuar will take over management and ownership of Kapawi in 2011.**

Further information: www.kapawi.com

WHEN TO GO

It can rain at any time in the Amazon, but the wettest months are February through to May. However, these are also the best months for wildlife viewing.

GETTING THERE

Kapawi is incredibly remote and can only be accessed by plane. From the Ecuadorian capital of Quito, a flight of half an hour takes you to the village of Coca where passengers board a smaller plane for an hour-long flight to Kapawi airstrip. From the airstrip it is a short hike and boat ride to the lodge – staff are there to help carry luggage.

Flights to Kapawi depart on Monday and Friday, so guests have the option to stay for either three, four or seven nights. Flights in and out are weather dependent (best to have a spare day in Quito at the end of your trip) and cost US$200 per person.

Kapawi has 20 double or triple rooms, each with their own bathroom, solar-heated shower and solar-powered lighting.

A three-night stay at Kapawi costs US$875 per person. Everything is included except alcohol, souvenirs and airport taxes.

FACING PAGE: While traditional Achuar culture is thriving, they're not averse to drawing on Western culture for useful attire such as T-shirts and backpacks!

GUATEMALA ~ ANTIGUA: THE HANDS-ON WAY TO LEARN SPANISH

BY ALEXANDRA GRAY

GREG JOHNSTON LPI

Spanish: the language of love and romance is also the language of nursery rhymes and blowing bubbles…well, that was my experience in Guatemala. The colonial town of Antigua has long been a mecca for travellers looking to do some intensive Spanish study, but it's also a great launch pad for getting involved in the local community – and expanding your Spanish repertoire at the same time!

I volunteered to assist the ever-growing class of four- and five-year-olds in Jochentenango, a small village northwest of Antigua. The school, Primeria Escuela Esperanza (First School of Hope), was established around Christmas 2004 by a 21-year-old Englishwoman from Nottingham. I was one of the first volunteers on board. The 200 or so students, ranging in age from four to 18 years, are provided with education and two meals a day. La Union, one of more than 70 Spanish-language schools in Antigua, donates funds towards the school and also provides volunteers to help with the workload.

The process to volunteer at a school or other organisation is really quite simple. Most of the Spanish-language schools are involved in several ongoing volunteer projects, ranging from schools and orphanages to farming or reforestation. The schools also link you up with a host family to live with, along with up to six other students also studying at the same school. This gives you a wonderful insight into life in Antigua – a town of 40,000 people interwoven with Mayan traditions and European cosmopolitan culture. It also provides a great support network of travelling buddies and the opportunity to further practise your Spanish by speaking with your host family.

On a typical day, I'd wake and be greeted by my host mother and our cook as I made my way to the shower. Breakfast was eggs with refried beans and fruit on the side, before heading off on a pleasant cobblestoned walk via the local markets to the central bus station. When the bus was handsomely full, we'd bump our way through the narrow streets to school.

I'd be greeted by tiny smiling faces welcoming me into the classroom at 8am. After some cutting and pasting, colouring in, ball games and singing songs, we'd break for playtime and eat food prepared by aproned mothers in a small canteen.

On one occasion, standing atop an old timber bench seat, I blew soap bubbles as children's eyes lit up, and they jumped and jostled to burst them. It was the best $2 that I ever spent. Following the break I would teach the children nursery rhymes in English or read a Spanish storybook that my language teacher would help me translate. English storybooks are a rare and cherished gift for these children, along with pens, pencils, colouring-in books and balls.

Leaving around lunchtime, I would be blown kisses and get hugs all round in an attempt to keep me there all day, but I had to attend language classes for four hours each afternoon. A bus trip back to town for my private lessons on a covered Colonial patio sitting opposite my teacher at a small wooden desk. Sometimes we would visit galleries or local markets to build my Spanish vocabulary or chat over coffee and cake in one of the many patisseries.

On my days off, the language school offered activities for students, which included climbing volcanoes, guided cycling tours to visit churches and historical places, and learning how to make tortillas.

RESPONSIBLE TRAVEL CREDENTIALS

- **Schools, hospitals, orphanages and other organisations in Guatemala simply don't have the human or financial resources to cope with community demand, so any assistance – skilled or unskilled – from travellers is enormously appreciated.**

- **Immersing yourself in the community is the best and quickest way to learn a language – and a wonderful forum for breaking down cross-cultural barriers!**

WHEN TO GO

Year-round. Peak season is from Christmas to Easter during the dry season. The wet season runs from April to early December – expect an afternoon downpour, and occasionally a day or two of soaking rain.

GETTING THERE

There are numerous international volunteers organisations that can arrange placements, you can contact a school directly before you arrive, or you can turn up and easily find a (locally-owned) Spanish school and affiliated volunteer programme.

If you arrange your stay in advance, you're looking at US$200 per week, which covers tuition, home-stay and extracurricular activities.

Further information: www.123teachme.com

Volunteering

One of the fundamentals of responsible tourism is 'giving something back' or making a personal, positive contribution to the people and places you're visiting. One of the best ways to do this is by volunteering – in fact, the 'voluntourism' phenomenon is rocking the travel world and there are now thousands of organised ways you can lend a hand to contribute to the world's wellbeing. The rewards – both for yourself and the people or ecosystems you are helping – can be enormous. You can volunteer with a conservation or cultural project virtually anywhere on the planet for anywhere from a weekend to a year or more. You might use your existing professional skills or you might uncover a latent Attenborough gene and discover the naturalist within.

We've included a range of short to medium-term volunteer projects in this book, none of which require any previous experience – all training is provided and you can find yourself doing anything from counting macaws *en masse* to inspecting parts of a turtle it would rather keep private. Many of the short-term volunteer projects and organisations such as Earthwatch Institute and Biosphere Expeditions, and the National Parks–associated projects, are predominantly conservation focused. Cultural- and community-focused projects tend to require a longer commitment because the project's success relies on the continuity of relationships between local people and volunteers. However this is not always the case.

Gap-year travellers are leading the charge on longer-term volunteering and a huge international business has sprung up to cater for the demand. Many gappers, career-breakers and others choose to volunteer abroad as an alternative way to travel. By staying in one place and interacting with local people, you will learn far more about the local culture and form genuine friendships. You will also develop new skills for overcoming the challenges life throws at you – day-to-day office problems can seem pretty insignificant when you have built a school with your bare hands!

There's more to volunteering than just turning up with a spade and asking where to dig. You'll be expected to put in long days working in challenging and unfamiliar surroundings. Living conditions can be basic, without running water or electricity and you must be prepared to cover most of your own expenses – development and conservation projects rely heavily on paying volunteers.

Understandably, not every would-be volunteer has what it takes. That said, the most important attribute that most organisations are looking for is a positive attitude and a genuine desire to help. Anyone who can speak English has the skills required to become an English teacher and anyone who can hold a hammer can help to build a community centre.

The overwhelming majority of longer-term (such as gap year) volunteer placements are arranged through sending agencies, which assess potential volunteers and place people on suitable projects around the world. These organisations work a little like temping agencies, matching volunteers to projects that need their specific skills and experience. Most placements involve community-development projects and humanitarian relief, providing hands-on help to impoverished and disadvantaged communities.

There are also smaller non-profit organisations that place volunteers alone or in pairs on small grass-roots projects. One advantage of going through a small or grass-roots operator is that the projects focus entirely on the local community. A common criticism of large volunteering organisations is that the placements focus too much on personal development for participants and not enough on the people they are supposed to help.

If you would rather make your own arrangements, there are numerous websites that provide listings of volunteering opportunities worldwide and most have a searchable database so you can search for projects in a particular region or field.

The US National Park Service, the New Zealand Department of Conservation and the National Parks and Wildlife Service in Australia take on large numbers of international volunteers to monitor plant and animal populations, repair trails and notice boards, and guide visitors.

For more information on all these services, see the listings at the back of this book (p213). You can also get information and post a message on the Gap Year & RTW Travel and Living and Working Abroad branches of the Lonely Planet Thorn Tree (http://thorntree.lonelyplanet.com) and get hold of either *The Gap Year Book* or *The Career Break Book*, both by Lonely Planet.

MEXICO ~ BANDERAS BAY:
UNDERSTANDING THE WHALE'S TAIL
BY RICHARD FIELD

RALPH LEE HOPKINS | LPI

RALPH LEE HOPKINS / LPI

The warm, clear waters of Mexico's Banderas Bay have long been an important breeding and calving ground for humpback whales. Every December roughly 300 of these giants spend the northern winter in the bay before starting their return journey in April. The arrival of the whales means big business for the people living on the bay, but for one company, it also means the resumption of a decade-long research project.

Ecotours de Mexico is one of the original whale-watching companies in Banderas Bay, and the longevity of this family-run operation could well be attributed to its sincere care and passion for the humpbacks. In 1996 Astrid Frisch, co-owner of Ecotours, began taking photographs of the unique patterns on the humpbacks' tail flukes so that she could begin to identify some of the regular visitors. What began as a hobby has resulted in the 'Photo-identification of Humpback Whales in Banderas Bay' catalogue.

From the catalogue, researchers are gaining valuable information relating to population numbers, migration behaviour, human impacts, climatic impacts and much more. The project has now expanded with several other companies involved and over 600 whales on the project's database. Astrid, the head researcher for the project, has also expanded her knowledge and is now doing biopsies on live whales to learn more about their genetics, food and toxins.

Visitors can assist the project in two ways. Firstly they can pay a small fee and 'adopt' a whale. The money from the adoption programme helps to support the photo-ID project. In return they receive a package that includes colour photos of 'their' whale, the history of the whale in Banderas Bay, and an adoption certificate. Alternatively, if guests take photographs of the necessary quality, they can send the photo to Ecotours where it will go into the database with their name attached.

Ecotours' guests leave with a massive understanding of humpbacks, but more importantly, they to get to know the whales personally. With humpbacks continually getting caught in nets, and whaling still making international headlines, there can be no better way to make people care for these gentle giants.

RESPONSIBLE TRAVEL CREDENTIALS

- **By respecting the whale-watching restrictions and actively encouraging other companies to do the same, Ecotours helps minimise stress on the whales, and assists in making the industry sustainable. The research done from the Ecotours boats is providing information valuable to the conservation of humpback whales.**

- **Ecotours is a small family-run business. It employs, educates and trains members of its local community to work as guides on its whale-watching boats. It supports the fishing community of Punta Mita.**

WHEN TO GO

The whale-watching season in Banderas Bay runs from mid-December to the end of March.

GETTING THERE

Puerto Vallarta can be reached by bus, car or plane. From Mexico City the bus trip takes around 12 hours while a flight takes one hour and costs between US$300 and US$400.

Puerto Vallarta has a wide range of accommodation catering for all budgets.

A half-day cruise includes transport, whale-watching, snorkelling at the Marietas Islands, lunch and soft drinks, and costs US$80 for adults and US$50 for children.

THIS PAGE: Breaching humpbacks can launch their 15m, 40-tonne body fully clear of the water.

FACING PAGE: While boats keep their required distance, the whales are notoriously curious and may approach close to the boat.

NETHERLANDS ANTILLES ~ SINT EUSTATIUS: MIRED IN HISTORY & NATURE

BY ALEX LEVITON

MARK WEBSTER | LPI

MARK WEBSTER | LPI

I s there really an island in the Caribbean with nary a resort, casino, cruise ship or chain restaurant, and just a handful of relaxed hotels? Except for dive aficionados and hikers, very few readers will recognise the official name – Sint Eustatius – and even fewer readers will know its more common nickname: Statia. The island had one of the busiest ports in the region during the 1700s and 1800s as ships trading in supplies from the Old World or slaves from Africa stopped in on the way to the colonies in America. These days, the island is mired in history and nature, with colonial ruins along the coast, a trail system heading up to a dormant volcano and 34 dive sites, including several sunken merchant ships offering an underwater archaeological treasure-trove.

The non-profit Stenapa (St Eustatius National Parks Foundation) is the organisation responsible for maintaining the pristine condition of the island. Stenapa manages the island's three park categories: the marine park, national park and botanical gardens. Stenapa itself runs an internship programme, while Working Abroad runs a two-month volunteer programme.

Three interns help oversee the different park divisions and stay at least four to six months. Depending on previous experience and skills, interns might be called upon to create hiking trails, educate local children, maintain sea moorings or landscape the botanical gardens. Volunteers might find themselves monitoring sea turtles overnight, helping with trail maintenance or keeping the island's roaming herds of goats and cows from dining in the botanical gardens.

Statia is not the place to come for partying, as the sea turtles and locals vie for the most relaxed pace of life. Both interns and volunteers have plenty of free time to dive, explore the island and take trips to the nearby islands of Saba and St Kitts. A popular activity is searching for the 'blue beads' that slaves used as currency. Visitors who find them washed up on shore or at a dive site are welcome to take them home as a reminder of their time on Statia.

RESPONSIBLE TRAVEL CREDENTIALS

- **The botanical gardens uses solar and wind power for electricity, and most of Statia's water supply is collected from rooftop cisterns.**

- **With only around 3000 full-time residents, volunteers and interns are assimilated quickly into this tightknit but friendly community. Interns and volunteers work and play alongside Statians and help educate local school children.**

- **The non-profit park system is entirely run by donations, grants and volunteers, with a small government subsidy. Every restaurant and hotel on Statia is locally owned or run, so most of the money volunteers spend stays on the island.**

WHEN TO GO

Sint Eustatius has pleasant weather all year-round and a mild rainy season from June to November. Turtle monitoring runs from March to November.

GETTING THERE

The only way to get to Statia is to take a Winair flight from St Martin for about US$100 round-trip.

Interns share a home at the botanical gardens and are provided with a full kitchen, bed and a truck or jeep for getting around the island. Bring bed linen and a mosquito net. Volunteers usually camp at the gardens and share the interns' kitchen and bathroom, and need to bring a tent.

Interns preferably possess such skills such as trail management, botany, or PADI Rescue level certification. Volunteers are simply required to be physically fit with a good work ethic.

The cost for volunteers is £978, which covers all costs for food, housing, transport etc for two months. There is no cost for the intern programme, but interns are required to take on much more responsibility and usually stay at least six months.

PERU ~ RIVER PIEDRAS:
DEEP IN THE PERUVIAN AMAZON
BY KERRY LORIMER

ALFREDO MARQUEZ | LPI

A dozen years ago I sat in a floating hide in the middle of a swiftly flowing river deep in the Peruvian Amazon, transfixed by a crimson blur.

About 15m away, a flock of scarlet macaws descended on the riverbank in a frenzy of feathers and flapping wings. They were so densely packed, it was difficult to distinguish individuals – but I counted at least 120.

Elsewhere on the river, I saw similar flocks of blue-and-yellow macaws and dusky headed parakeets. Above, howler monkeys whooped and swung through the canopy and toucans looped their beak-heavy flight across a slice of sky hemmed by impenetrable jungle.

No-one really knows why the birds – not just macaws, but parrots and also mammals – congregate en masse on the 'clay licks' (colpas), on the riverbanks of Peru's Tambopata region. Scientists speculate that the clay counteracts toxins from poisonous fruits and seeds ingested by the animals. Whatever the reason, it makes for one of the world's most colourfully profuse wildlife spectacles.

In the years since my parrot epiphany, farming, tourism, logging and other pressures have increasingly encroached on the jungle. In Peru, thankfully, large tracts have been hived off into protected reserves, among them the Manu and Tambopata reserves, both of which hold world records for biodiversity.

The adjacent River Piedras system connects Tambopata and Manu. It is equally diverse and important, but it is not protected – although a lot of scientists and conservationists believe it should be.

Enter Biosphere Expeditions – and a posse of willing volunteers. Teams of paying volunteers are collecting data to present a case for formally protecting the Piedras rainforest. A typical expedition day might involve walking with a partner through the forest, tracking, spotting and noting animal and bird species along the way: but you'll have to write quickly to keep up! The forest is jumping with various monkey species, including Capuchins and howlers; peccaries, ocelots, tapirs and deer; dozens of species of birds – even jaguar.

You'll climb to platforms in the canopy to observe monkeys and birds and take night walks where you'll learn the difference between the red-coal eyes of a nocturnal cat and those of a caiman.

And best of all, you'll get to sit in a hide on the river and count the birds, and to hear the sound – like river rapids – as they lift off as one and swoop away.

RESPONSIBLE TRAVEL CREDENTIALS

- **The Manu/Tambopata area is the largest uninhabited tract of rainforest on earth. The research expedition's aim is to collect enough data to inform decision-makers to enable the creation of a private protected reserve.**

- **Biosphere Expeditions offsets the carbon debt incurred by its field operations.**

- **At the conclusion of the expedition, Biosphere produces a report detailing the scientific results, which is distributed to participants as well as made public through academia and the media.**

- **Biosphere Expeditions is a non-profit organisation. Two thirds of the expedition cost goes directly towards funding the research project.**

WHEN TO GO

The expeditions are held during the dry season – which is still fairly wet – in May and June. Subtropical temperatures can range up to 35°C.

GETTING THERE

The research area is located on a remote stretch of the River Piedras, around seven hours from Puerto Maldonado, the assembly point for the expedition. There are flights to Puerto Maldonado from either Lima or Cusco, and the Biosphere Expeditions team will transport you by boat to the research site.

Base camp is basic but comfortable twin-share accommodation in a lodge built from local materials. All meals are included.

No special skills are required – training will be provided, but you do need to be reasonably fit.

The expeditions run for two-week, back-to-back periods.

Participation costs £1100 for the 13-day expedition (departing Puerto Maldonado) and teams are limited to 10 people.

VENEZUELA ~ SANTA ELENA DE UAIRÉN: VOLUNTEER ADVENTURES

BY DEBRA HERRMANN

Volunteering – thought it through, decided it wasn't for you? Don't have the time, money or skills? Besides, it can't be both exotic and easy?

Santa Elena de Uairén, Venezuela, near the border of Brazil and Guyana: picture forest bordering on highland savanna; a mild, dry climate that curtails tropical nasties; birdsong and monkey calls for your listening pleasure. You need only work five hours a day, doing what you prefer to do, learn a new language if you choose and, in your spare time, explore some of the oldest terrain on the planet. All while preserving the local ecology and making a difference to the lives of the Pemón indigenous community.

Practically all ages, abilities and interests are catered for in the volunteer programme at Santa Elena. Projects include conservation work in re-forestation and seedling propagation, sustainable agriculture and building projects, tour guiding, landscaping and woodwork – volunteers can work on single or combined projects. Among the options for the indoors-oriented, there's English or assistant teaching, caring for kids with special needs and the preparation of learning aids or play equipment. Skilled placements such as physiotherapy, psychology and occupational therapy are also offered. Costs are very low when compared with similar programmes and the minimum commitment required is a mere three days.

Home-stays with local families can be arranged. There's also a volunteer guesthouse if you prefer an independent self-catering alternative. English, Spanish and German are spoken. Spanish classes are available to volunteers at minimal cost.

KRZYSZTOF DYDYNSKI LPI

RESPONSIBLE TRAVEL CREDENTIALS

- **Health and educational programmes allow volunteers to contribute directly to the well-being of local communities. Agricultural and building projects based in Pemón villages are cooperative ventures planned and conducted with cultural sensitivity as a primary concern.**

- **Through a range of conservation projects volunteers are encouraged to actively contribute to preserving the local ecology. Recommended tour providers are chosen for their environmentally responsible tourism practices.**

- **Aside from being a forum for valuable cultural exchange, Spanish classes and home-stays provide jobs and other economic benefits for the local community.**

WHEN TO GO

With southern Venezuela's mild climate and the large range of volunteer projects on offer, volunteering in Santa Elena is possible at any time of year. Check with a programme coordinator for the best time for the project of your choice. Outdoor work may be easier in the dry season (November to May).

GETTING THERE

Santa Elena de Uairén can be reached by regular bus services or flight connections from Caracas or regional centres such as Ciudad Bolívar or Puerto Ordaz. A transfer service is also available to assist with bookings and flight connections.

You can stay in a self-catering guesthouse or with a family home-stay.

FACING PAGE: If you're arranging a volunteer placement, it's worth visiting Angel Falls – the world's highest at 979m – while you're in the area. Eco-tours of the falls are available.

KRZYSZTOF DYDYNSKI LPI

Responsible Tourism: The Big Picture

Each year over 700 million people travel internationally. By 2020 it's estimated 1.5 billion will be hitting the road. It's not hard to imagine how this runaway juggernaut, barrelling on out of control, will result in wilderness destroyed (made way for 'tourism infrastructure' or trampled into oblivion), species extinction and traditional cultures lost or disenfranchised.

Tourism – done right – can be a powerful tool for conserving wilderness and heritage areas. For both traveller and local, it increases appreciation of the spiritual and environmental importance of conserving biodiversity.

More than that, if governments and local people can see that wildlife and wild areas have a monetary value, it's a pretty strong incentive not to destroy them for short-term gains: you can only kill a gorilla once, but if you can keep it alive, it can earn your country US$90,000 every year, year after year, through tourism. The same goes for cultural heritage such as buildings, traditions and artisan skills.

And think about it: how far would greater cross-cultural understanding go towards solving the problems of our world? Humankind's innate curiosity fuels our interest in learning about other cultures. Urbanised Westerners are drawn to alternative lifestyles, tribal societies and different value systems and traditions. Equally, 'traditional' cultures take their cues from the West for their own future development. Responsible travel aims to facilitate authentic, meaningful interactions between traveller and local – where each may learn from the other, where the exchange is equal rather than exploitative and fosters greater understanding on both sides.

It's an idealistic concept, true. And sometimes travellers' expectations of 'authenticity' will be at odds with the local peoples' desires to simply make a buck. Its success is, to a degree, dependent on travellers accepting that even 'traditional'

cultures aren't static, but are constantly evolving, and that the members of those cultures have the right to determine the direction of that evolution.

Responsible tourism can help to put a value on traditional wisdom and livelihoods as well as offering alternative, supplementary sources of income that allow – and encourage – the traditional ways to be sustained. In many impoverished communities, this is also a means of stemming the loss to urban areas of young people seeking work: if they can earn a living back home, traditions are more likely to be maintained across generations and the social fabric of the community remains intact.

One of the best ways to help alleviate poverty is to travel.

From an economic perspective, as the world's largest industry, tourism has a profound potential to reduce poverty. But again, it needs to be done right.

In many countries, particularly in the developing world, the purse strings of the tourism industry are held by big – often foreign-owned – business. The huge revenues of five-star, multinational hotels rarely trickle down to benefit the people of the host country. Instead, they're spirited off-shore and in many cases, where the local government or community is forced to fund supporting infrastructure such as roads and utilities, the host country actually ends up *paying* for the privilege of putting up the foreign tourists.

The responsible tourism model looks at ways of channelling tourist funds into the local community in the most direct way possible and to best effect. Ways in which this can happen include 'community-based' tourism – usually small, grass-roots, locally owned operatives providing tours, accommodation and other services. Some of the extraordinary examples in this book include Ulu Ai in Borneo, township tourism in South Africa and Chalalan lodge in Bolivia. And there are more starting up all over the world.

A second way is through a partnership with a larger, more experienced operator or NGO which can bring business skills and financial support to the community initiative. This is quite common in Africa – Damaraland Camp in Namibia and Nkwichi Lodge in Mozambique are good examples.

The next level up is the foreign-based responsible tourism operator, whose responsible tourism policy prescribes staying in locally owned accommodation, employing local guides and staff, sourcing supplies locally and, perhaps, funding an environmental initiative or donating a portion of each passenger's tour to their host communities.

Is responsible travel the way of the future?

Let's hope so.

Unless we do make a paradigm shift in our attitudes to tourism and travel we'll lose the wild places, the traditions and eccentricities of the world – life will be far more homogenised and far less surprising, and our spirit will be the poorer for it.

Responsible tourism is not a panacea, nor is it the full or only answer. There are substantial risks, particularly where the 'eco' label is bandied about but not genuinely applied. Tourism of any kind inevitably makes an impact – the challenge is in sustainably managing the negative and reaping the benefits of the positive.

Travelling 'responsibly' is a step in the right direction.

So there you have it. Travelling by the responsible travel ethos is one of the most direct and personal ways you can make a difference to some of the biggest issues affecting our world: poverty and peace. And you'll have the time of your life doing it.

Lonely Planet Foundation: Widely, Lightly, Sustainably

Travel widely, tread lightly, give sustainably: this is the mission of the Lonely Planet Foundation. You can hear us murmuring this mantra as we wander around the office with itchy feet aching to get back on the road. As passionate travellers we are working to give back to the world we love exploring by making tangible, positive differences at home and abroad.

Since the Foundation's launch in March 2005, we have committed to putting 5% of Lonely Planet's annual profit towards supporting a wide variety of grass-roots charities around the globe. We figure it makes sense to do what we can to give back to the incredible places that have inspired us for so many years.

So what's the Foundation all about?

We're about supporting sustainable, grass-roots organisations, predominately in the developing world, that empower the community and have long-term benefits. The charities we support focus first and foremost on health and education and, secondarily, on conservation and environmentalism. We are committed to supporting projects that empower women to improve their local community, as well as projects with an emphasis on child health, education and civil rights.

We are also excited to support projects that maintain or foster the positive attributes of tourism and the respectful preservation of tourist areas and the environment. After all, we want these spectacular ancient sites and natural wonders to be around so locals and travellers alike can enjoy them for a good long time to come.

For these reasons, we decided to support a remarkable project to excavate a minaret in remote southwestern Afghanistan, while shielding the site from looters, to help give local people a sustainable source of income from intrepid travellers who will come to visit this amazing location.

The Foundation has also supported the following varied projects around the world:

- Practical empowerment and humanitarian assistance for women in East Timor

- A numeracy and literacy training centre for underprivileged children in Swaziland

- Working to create long-term sources of safe water for people throughout sub-Saharan Africa and south Asia

- Vocational training for street children and disadvantaged youth in Vietnam

See www.lonelyplanet.com/foundation for more information.

Useful Organisations Index

Carbon Neutral
(www.carbonneutral.com.au)
A carbon-offset programme for travellers and businesses.

CarbonNeutral Company
(www.carbonneutral.com) A scheme whereby travellers can pay for trees to be planted to counter travel-related carbon emissions.

CITES (Convention on International Trade in Endangered Species)
(www.cites.org) Listings of the world's endangered species and background information on travel-related issues.

Climate Care
(www.co2.org) A 'pay as you pollute' scheme offsetting businesses' and travellers' carbon emissions (from air/land travel and production) by funding projects promoting renewable energy, energy efficiency and forest restoration.

Department for International Development
(www.dfid.gov.uk) UK-based; profiles and background information on developing countries and work towards poverty elimination.

ecotravel.com
(www.ecotravel.com) Directory of responsible-tourism holidays worldwide.

ECPAT (Child Wise in Australia)
(www.ecpat.org) A charity working to end child prostitution, pornography and trafficking, including child sex tourism.

ethicalescape
(www.ethicalescape.co.uk) Online directory of ecotravel products worldwide.

Green Globe 21
(www.greenglobe21.com) A worldwide certification scheme for responsible-tourism operators, backed by the UN (qualified operators exhibit the Green Globe logo).

International Centre for Responsible Tourism (ICRT)
(www.icrtourism.org) Based at Greenwich University (UK); has information on responsible tourism and educational opportunities.

International Ecotourism Society (TIES)
(www.ecotourism.org) Largest responsible-tourism organisation dedicated to generating and disseminating information on responsible tourism. Also has an online library.

Nature Conservancy (TNC)
(www.nature.org/ecotourism) US-based conservation NGO that also offers travel and volunteering programmes.

Nepal Mountaineering Association
(www.nma.com.np) Apply here for climbing and remote-area permits.

Pro-Poor Tourism
(www.propoortourism.org.uk) Information on Pro-Poor Tourism: tourism that creates net benefits for poor people.

responsibletravel.com
(www.responsibletravel.com) Excellent online travel agency detailing responsible travel holidays worldwide.

Sustainable Travel International
(www.sustainabletravelinternational.org) US-based comprehensive resource on responsible travel including travel directory, study opportunities, eco-certification.

Tourism Concern
(www.tourismconcern.org.uk) UK-based organisation campaigning for fair and ethically-traded tourism. Publishes *The Good Alternative Travel Guide* (Earthscan, 2002), a comprehensive listing of worldwide community-based tourism projects, and follow-on *The Ethical Travel Guide* (Earthscan, 2006).

Tourism for Tomorrow Awards
(www.tourismfortomorrow.com) Most prestigious international awards recognising excellence in responsible tourism development. Information on past winners is listed on the site.

Travelroots
(www.travelroots.com) Online travel agency listing responsible tourism holidays.

UN Environment Programme
(www.uneptie.org/pc/tourism/ecotourism) The sustainable tourism domain of the UN Environment Programme.

World Tourism Organisation
(www.world-tourism.org) UN agency serving as a forum for tourism policy issues and a practical information resource.

World Travel & Tourism Council
(www.wttc.org) Background on international issues, agreements and useful links.

Worldwide Fund for Nature (WWF)
(www.panda.org) Global environmental conservation organisation. Site has information on sustainable tourism and offers responsible-tourism holidays.

Operator Index

ACTED Murghab
www.acted.org

Adventure Company
www.adventurecompany.co.uk

Africa Calling
www.africacalling.com

Africa in Focus
www.africainfocus.com

Al Maha Desert Resort
www.al-maha.com

Alternative Hawaii
www.alternative-hawaii.com

Anangu Tours
www.anangutours.com.au

Andean Trails
www.andeantrails.co.uk

Another Way Travel
www.anotherwaytravel.com

Arnhem Land Safaris
www.arnhemland-safaris.com

Atauro Island, Tua Koin Resort
www.atauroisland.com

ATG Oxford
www.atg-oxford.co.uk

Badawiya Hotel and Safari
www.badawiya.com

Baikal Watch
www.earthisland.org

Biosphere Expeditions
www.biosphere-expeditions.org

Birding Africa
www.birding-africa.com

Birdlife International
www.birdlife.org

BlueGreen Adventures
www.bluegreenadventures.com

Borneo Adventure
www.borneoadventure.com

Bush and Beyond Guided Trekking
www.naturetreks.co.nz

C2C Guide
www.c2c-guide.co.uk

Carpathian Large Carnivore Project
www.clcp.ro

Chalalan Lodge
www.chalalan.com in Spanish

Chumbe Island Lodge
www.chumbeisland.com

Classic Safari Company
www.classicsafaricompany.com.au

Community Based Tourism Kyrgystan
www.cbtkyrgyzstan.kg

Conservation International
www.ecotour.org

Council Exchanges
www.councilexchanges.org

Cultural Restoration Tourism Project
www.crtp.net

Culture Xplorers
www.cultureexplorers.com

Damaraland Camp
www.wilderness-safaris.com

Danube Delta Tours
www.danubedeltatours.ro

Day Trippers
www.daytrippers.co.za

Discovery Initiatives
www.discoveryinitiatives.co.uk

Djembelfaq Drums
http://djembelfaq.drums.org

Dragoman
www.dragoman.co.uk

Earthwatch Institute (Europe)
www.earthwatch.org

Ecotours Vallarta
www.ecotoursvallarta.com

Elder Hostel
www.elderhostel.org

Exodus Travels
www.exodus.co.uk

Explore Worldwide
www.exploreworldwide.com

Federated Mountain Clubs of New Zealand
www.fmc.org.nz

Frontiers Foundation
www.frontiersfoundation.ca

FSM Tourism
www.visit-fsm.org

Fundación Aldeas de Paz (Peace Villages Foundation)
www.peacevillages.org

GAP Adventures
www.gapadventures.com

Gecko's Adventures
www.geckosadventures.com

Geocities Otonga Adventure Tours
www.geocities.com/toguna_adventure_tours

Ger to Ger Expeditions
www.gertoger.com

Global Resource Action Center for the Environment
www.gracelinks.org

Global Security Institute
www.gsinstitute.org/gsi/index.html

Global Tiger Patrol
www.globaltigerpatrol.co.uk

Grand Canyon National Park
www.nps.gov/grca

Grassroute Tours
www.grassroutetours.co.za

Great Excursions
www.greatexcursions.com

Guerba
www.guerba.co.uk

Historic Route 66
www.historic66.com

Idealist.org
www.idealist.org

Imaginative Traveller
www.imaginative-traveller.com

International Association of Antarctic Tour Operators
www.iaato.org

International Association of Lawyers Against Nuclear Arms
www.ialana.net/home.htm

International Galapagos Tour Operators Association
www.igtoa.org

International Sivananda Yoga Vedanta Centres
www.sivananda.org

Into Africa
www.intoafrica.co.uk

Intrepid Travel
www.intrepidtravel.com

Kaikoura Information & Tourism Inc www.kaikoura.co.nz

Kapawi: Amazon Ecolodge and Reserve
www.kapawi.com

Kasbah du Toubkal
www.kasbahdutoubkal.com

Kayak Bahamas
www.kayakbahamas.com

Kayak Sydney
www.kayaksydney.com

Kyrgyz Community Based Tourism Association 'Hospitality Kyrgyzstan'
www.cbtkyrgyzstan.kg

Languages Abroad
www.languagesabroad.com

Linbald Expeditions
www.expeditions.com

Llama Treks and Llama Pack Trips
www.llamapack.com

Lord Howe Island Tourist Commission
www.lordhoweisland.info

Mahout
www.mahoutuk.com

Maine Windjammer Association
www.sailmainecoast.com

Manda Nkwichi Lodge
www.mandawilderness.org

Mountain Travel Sobek US
www.mtsobek.com

Mountains Tours Office Trekking in Sinai
www.sheikmousa.com

Nature Conservancy (TNC)
www.nature.org/ecotourism

Nature Trek
www.naturetreks.co.nk

Nigaloo Blue
www.ningalooblue.com.au

NPS VIP Program
www.nps.gov/volunteer

Okinawa Tourist Information
www.ocvb.or.jp

Omapere Tourist Hotel
www.omapere.co.nz

Outdoor Finland
www.luontoon.fi

Pacific Northwest Expeditions Ltd
www.seakayak.com

Peregrine Adventures
www.peregrineadventures.com

Point Afrique Charter Flights
www.point-afrique.com

Rainbow Tours
www.rainbowtours.co.uk

Ramblers
www.ramblers.org.uk

Real Africa
www.realafrica.co.uk

Route 66 Guide
www.national66.com

Royal Society for the Conservation of Nature (RSCN) Jordan
www.rscn.org.jo

Samburu Trails Trekking Safaris
www.samburutrails.com

Sea Kayak British Columbia
www.seakayakbc.com

Service Civil International
www.sciint.org

Sierra Club
www.sierraclub.org

Southern Sea Ventures
www.southernseaventures.com

Sunvil Africa
www.sunvil.co.uk

Sustrans Organisation
www.sustrans.org.uk

Tarkine Trails
www.tasmaniawalks.com

Tonga Holidays
www.tongaholiday.com

Tread Lightly
www.treadlightly.com

Trek Larapinta
www.treklarapinta.com.au

Tribal Warrior Association
www.tribalwarrior.org

Tribes Fair Trade Travel
www.tribes.co.uk

Trips Worldwide
www.tripsworldwide.co.uk

Tropical Ecological Adventures
www.tropiceco.com

Tua Koin Resort, Atauro Island
www.atauroisland.com

Tucan Travel
www.tucantravel.com

UCOTA
www.ucota.or.ug

Volunteer International
www.volunteerinternational.com

Web Walking
www.webwalking.com/hike.shtml

Whale Swim Adventures
www.whaleswim.com

Whalewatch New Zealand
www.whalewatch.co.nz

Wild Animal Rescue Foundation of Thailand
www.warthai.org

Wilderness Travel
www.wildernesstravel.com

Women's International League for Peace and Freedom
www.reachingcriticalwill.org

Working Abroad
www.workingabroad.com

World Endeavours
www.worldendeavors.com

World Expeditions
www.worldexpeditions.com.au

Yangphel Adventure Travel
www.yangphel.com

Yellowstone National Park
www.nps.gov/yell

Youth for Understanding
www.yfu.org

Volunteer Organisations

There are literally thousands of volunteer organisations around the world, catering for everyone from unskilled holiday-makers who want to spend some time helping on a local project, to gap-year and career-break travellers, to specialist professionals prepared to dedicate years to a cause. Projects range from humanitarian aid to conservation research, archaeology digs to teaching English – and you can get involved in just about any country you care to name. For a much more comprehensive range of volunteering opportunities, get hold of Lonely Planet's *The Career Break Book* or *The Gap Year Book*.

In addition to the organisations already mentioned in this book the following organisations offer projects that blend volunteering with travelling/holiday-making: they offer short-term projects that don't require specialised skills.

Scientific & Conservation Projects

BTCV International Conservation Holidays
www.btcv.org

Coral Cay Conservation
www.coralcay.org

Ecovolunteers (WildWings/ WildOceans)
www.ecovolunteer.org.uk
www.wildwings.co.uk

Frontier
www.frontierprojects.ac.uk

Global Vision International (GVI)
www.gvi.co.uk

Greenforce
www.greenforce.org

Oceanic Society
www.oceanic-society.org

Operation Wallacea
www.opwall.com

People's Trust for Endangered Species (PTES)
www.ptes.org

Rainforest Concern
www.rainforestconcern.org

Scientific Exploration Society
www.ses-explore.org

World Wide Opportunities on Organic Farms (WWOOF)
www.wwoof.org.uk

Humanitarian Projects

AidCamps International
www.aidcamps.org

Amizade
www.amizade.org

Cross-Cultural Solutions
www.crossculturalsolutions.org

Global Crossroad
www.globalcrossroad.com

Global Volunteer Network
www.volunteer,org.nz

Global Volunteers
www.globalvolunteers.org

International Volunteers for Peace Australia
www.ivp.org.au

Involvement Volunteers Association
www.volunteering.org.au

i-to-i
www.i-to-i.com

Muir's Tours/Nepal Kingdom Foundation
www.nkf-mt.org.uk

Travellers Worldwide
www.travellersworldwide.com

UNA Exchange
www.unaexchange.org

Other

The following organisations provide listings of volunteering placements around the world for people who don't want to go through a mainstream volunteer organisation.

Action Without Borders
www.idealist.org

International Volunteer Programs Association (IVPA)
www.volunteerinternational.org

National Centre for Volunteering
www.volunteering.org.uk

Worldwide Volunteering
www.worldwidevolunteering.org.uk

Index

Code Green
Experiences of a Lifetime
May 2006

Published by
Lonely Planet Publications Pty Ltd
ABN 36 005 607 983
90 Maribyrnong St, Footscray,
Victoria, 3011, Australia
www.lonelyplanet.com

Printed through The Bookmaker International Ltd. Printed in China

Photographs
Many of the images in this book are available for licensing
from Lonely Planet Images (LPI).
www.lonelyplanetimages.com
ISBN 174104734X

Lonely Planet Offices

AUSTRALIA Locked Bag 1, Footscray, Victoria, 3011
Phone 03 8379 8000 Fax 03 8379 8111
Email talk2us@lonelyplanet.com.au

USA 150 Linden St, Oakland, CA 94607
Phone 510 893 8555 Toll free 800 275 8555 Fax 510 893 8572
Email info@lonelyplanet.com

UK 72-82 Rosebery Ave London EC1R 4RW
Phone 020 7841 9000 Fax 020 7841 9001
Email go@lonelyplanet.co.uk

Although the authors and Lonely Planet have taken all reasonable care in preparing
this book, we make no warranty about the accuracy or completeness of its content
and, to the maximum extent permitted, disclaim all liability from it's use.

Coordinating Author: Kerry Lorimer
Contributing Authors: Abigail Hole, Adam Long, Alex Leviton, Alexandra Gray,
Andrew Dean Nystrom, Anthony Sattin, Bradley Mayhew, Bridhe McGroder,
David Atkinson, Debra Herrmann, Don George, Emma Gilmour, Etain O'Carroll,
Ethan Gelber, Garry Weare, Giselle Radulovic, James Jeffrey, Jill Kirby, Joe Cawley,
Kerryn Burgess, Kris Madden, Mark Elliott, Philip Engelberts, Rachel Alt, Ray Bartlett,
Richard Field, Rod Griffith, Sam Benson, Sarah Wintle, Simon Richmond,
Simon Sellars, Tim Rock, Tom Hall, Tony Wheeler

Publisher: Roz Hopkins
Publishing Manager: Chris Rennie
Editorial & Production Manager: Jenny Bilos
Publishing Planning Manager: Jo Vraca
Creative Director: Jane Pennells
Designer: Daniel New
Design & Layout Assistance: Brendan Dempsey, Laura Jane & Jim Hsu
Editors: Martine Lleonart & Kyla Gillzan
Image Researchers: Kerry Lorimer, Chris Rennie & Daniel New
Cartographer: Wayne Murphy
Print Production: Graham Imeson
Pre-press Production: Ryan Evans

With many thanks to:
Ben Handicott, Jennifer Garrett, Fiona Siseman & Carol Chandler.